A Precious Walk with Jesus

Ron Johnson

1st Edition

Contents

Introduction

What Christians need now is a precious walk with my Jesus. Some people might think it is too late – *the world is too far gone and only God can straighten out this mess*. But I believe my Jesus is in the transforming business now more then ever and He wants us to use the power and authority He gave us. So let us get started.

I am blessed to have a special time with my Jesus everyday. I call this time *Coffee Time With Jesus*. People ask me how I got this way. I tell them I hear from God and not just in my special time but every minute of everyday.

Here is an example of talking to my Jesus and how my Jesus removed my fear. One morning while I'm having Coffee Time With Jesus; Jesus led me into Matthew 10:18-20.

Matthew 10:18-20 And ye shall be brought before governors and kings for my sake, for a testimony against them and the Gentiles. But when they deliver you up, take no thought how or what ye shall speak: for it shall be given you in that same hour what ye shall speak. For it is not ye that speak, but the Spirit of your Father which speaketh in you.

'For it is not ye that speak, but the Spirit of your Father which speaketh in you.' Do you hear the Words of my Jesus? These are His Words to us. Jesus will give us the words to help anyone come to know Him. I asked Jesus who is the magistrate to me. I have never been called before governors or kings so I ask my dearest Jesus who is the magistrate to me. Jesus said anyone I put before you. Jesus just took all the pressure off me or us talking to people about God. Jesus is my Protector and Jesus will give me the words to help anyone He puts in front of me. I don't have to worry for my Jesus will give me the words. I love you too, Jesus!

I pray that you are reading this book because you have a heart for God's creation. I assume you already know of God and would like to know Him more intimately. I believe a walk with God starts with knowing of Him. I don't believe we can come into an intimate relationship with any one we don't know or anyone we cannot hear from. Most people know of Jesus and probably think He is the guy that died for our sins and they are right. Jesus died for our sins but Jesus did so much more.

Jesus also came to enable us to have conversation with Him. In Genesis, we read where Jesus came in the cool of the day to talk to Adam and Eve. Shortly after Adam and Eve ate of the tree of knowledge of good and evil, Jesus stopped coming to talk to them. Conversation with God became very limited. It seems to me that only a few people actually had intimate conversation with God in the Old Testament.

When Jesus came He restored our broken relationship and He made communicating with Him a must. Think how hard it would be to fall in love with someone you could not talk to or hear from. Most of the people in the Old Testament know of God but it seems to me only a few know Him with the intimacy we (New Testament) believers have been granted.

I believe a walk with God starts with an awareness of maybe there is a God. Then comes the awareness of God and with that awareness comes a desire to fall in love with God. When people become aware of God they either reject Him because they think of Him as religion; rules and laws they don't want to be bothered with. Or they desire to know more about Him because they have heard some of the truth '*Jesus came to set us free.*'

They wonder how that happens. Then they will look to us believers in Jesus Christ to see if we live what we say we believe. We believers must live what we believe not just talk what we believe. True believers will walk in the same realm of belief Jesus walked in. This is important because people will watch you before they will ever listen to you. The realm of belief I am talking about is the realm of believing in His forgiveness, your worthiness, and through these gifts, believing in His love for you.

Usually these curious people will seek God through other people who seem to know God. Looking for God or the knowledge of God in others is actually a dangerous place to start your walk with the Lord. It is dangerous because unknowingly you might be putting your faith in a person and their knowledge of God and by doing so you are setting yourself up for disappointment. I say this because you are actually unknowingly putting your faith in a person and not God. At some point in your walk the person will probably disappoint you. Jesus tells us to simply seek ye first the kingdom of God with your whole heart, mind and soul by asking the Holy Spirit into your heart to dwell their. I pray to give you a desire to know Jesus more in this book and I pray you receive the desire to be intimately close to Jesus and not Ron Johnson.

As you read on you will see Jesus came to inspire us to know the Father through His life and His words. I believe we believers have the same commission as Jesus. We are to inspire people through our life and our transparent heart, to want, or seek the same relationship Jesus has with His Father. We do this by choosing to have the Holy Spirit of God live in us now.

Even Jesus did not want His disciples following Him as a man but instead Jesus wanted us to follow Him through the Holy Spirit. Jesus knew by coming to us in His Holy Spirit He would fulfill the scripture with His guarantee

Hebrews 13:5 Let your conduct *be* without covetousness; *be* content with such things as you have. For He Himself has said, "I will never leave you nor forsake you."

I love my Jesus and His guarantee, *"I will never leave you nor forsake you."* But wait, there is more! Jesus very plainly told the disciples in the book of John:

John 14:26 But the Helper, the Holy Spirit, whom the Father will send in My name, He will teach you all things, and bring to your remembrance all things that I said to you.

Yes, Jesus tells us His Holy Spirit is the Helper, the Comforter, the Savior and Jesus tells us He will never leave you or forsake you. These are the promises of God and the true gifts from

God. Knowing of and believing in these promises from God will change the way you think in your heart and they will renew you mind daily. These promises will allow you too walk with the Lord, intimately and believing in these promises will allow Jesus to give you His words to help others.

I am blessed to have what I call *Coffee Time With Jesus*. Simply put, I have intimate time with Jesus everyday. I know Jesus came to show us by example how to have an intimate relationship with Him. Jesus came and restored our communication with Him and gave us the Holy Spirit of Himself and Father God. They are the ultimate teachers and if you let them, they will dwell in you and they will teach you all things.

If we believe John 14:26, we will inherit the same commission Jesus volunteered for and when we believe we will receive the gifts of the Holy Spirit into our heart, so we will be equipped like Jesus was equipped. The Holy Spirit will talk through us and guide us. We will fulfill our commission – to inspire others to know God through our actions, our words and our life.

Please read on and you will find how believing in Jesus makes all things possible.

The First Step

Jesus tells us in His Word to *seek first the kingdom of God and His righteousness;* so that must be the first step.

Matthew 6:33 But seek first the kingdom of God and His righteousness, and all these things shall be added to you.

This is the starting point in our walk with the Lord and most Christians will tell you to start by reading and studying your Bible. I remember I started my walk by asking Christians, *"How or where do I start reading the Bible?"* I was told there are an old part and a new part. The people I talked to says to start at the beginning and read through the Bible like you would read just any other book. Being told to read the Bible was a good advice, for sure. But my problem is I am a very slow reader. If you are a slow reader, you too might find it hard to get through the Old Testament.

Personally I suggest reading Genesis first for Genesis is foundational. But please as you read Genesis don't try to figure out all the details. Your mind will go crazy trying to figure out creation. Simply read it and allow Jesus to prove it true to you personally by asking Him to talk to you personally. He will talk to you. I know because He said in His Word He is no respecter of persons which means He proved His Word true to me and He will prove it true to you.

After Genesis, I suggest you go right into the New Testament. I mean we live in the New Testament of having Jesus Christ as our Savior and King so you need to go there. Please remember the whole Bible is important, but I believe we start in the New Testament to learn how God deals with us today. The New Testament is the life we are to live today. Yes every one of us has the capability to live the love of Jesus today. Actually we are

5

commissioned to be witnesses of His love today. This may sound impossible but Jesus said that all things are possible for those that believe. Mark 9:23 is another foundational Scripture for us to simply ponder and Jesus will bring the truth of it into our heart.

Mark 9:23 Jesus said to him, "If you can believe, all things are possible to him who believes."

Jesus said if you can believe and I want to be the one who believes then all things are possible. I have made a choice to believe and if you want to believe ask my Jesus to help you understand this scripture and He will. I believe. Do you?

As you read your Holy Bible please ask Jesus to come into your heart and teach you about His kingdom and His righteousness. We ask Jesus into our heart to become like Jesus. In Genesis God said

Genesis 1:26 And God said, Let us make man in our image, after our likeness

Right in Genesis 1, we see we are to be the image of God on the earth and be in His likeness. This is important to understand we are to be like our Creator. Read on and you will see the image of God is love. But how do attain that image after the fall of man?

Jesus in His Word tells us that He is our Teacher. Friends have asked me what version of the Bible to read? I tell them if you ask Jesus Christ into your heart and ask Jesus to be your teacher, then Jesus will teach you and bring you into all truth. Jesus is the teacher of teachers. So put your trust in Him being your teacher and even if your translation isn't considered the best one, then guess what? With faith in Jesus being your teacher, you will still learn His truth. Jesus says in John 14:26:

John 14:26 But the Comforter, which is the Holy Ghost, whom the Father will send in my name, he shall teach you all things, and bring all things to your remembrance, whatsoever I have said unto you.

There are numerous places in His Holy Bible where Jesus refers to himself as our teacher. I chose John 14:26 as a reference because Jesus is talking about the future to the apostles and to us, His whole human race. I believe the best place to start in a relationship with God is to establish who the teacher is. Jesus made our life pretty simple by only giving us one book to study – *The Holy Bible*. Yes! We need His Holy Bible and we also need a teacher. Now that we know who our Teacher is – *Jesus Christ* and we have His Holy Bible, let us get going.

Oh yes, please don't read the Holy Bible to go through it in six months or any time frame. I don't believe Jesus has a time frame. I am asking you to please ask Jesus to teach you as you read His Holy Bible. This may seem a bit much at first but you will be putting your trust in Jesus and not man. You see, we believers are commissioned to help others come to know God by giving them a desire to know God but it is God who awakens His faith, His hope, and His joy in you as He shows you His undeniable love for you.

As you read His Word and if a Scripture pops out at you, then please know that you are hearing from God and dwell there for as long as it takes to let what God is impressing on your mind go into your heart. When you are ready, you will hear God tell you to move on. One of the most impressive moments in your life will be the day Jesus calls you by your name. If that hasn't happened yet, please open your mind enough to think of this possibility. The Creator of the universe knows your name and is anxiously waiting for you to open your heart to hear from Him.

I am writing this book but these are not my words. Jesus wants for you to come into His heart by your simple desire to know if He is real. Jesus is longing for you to desire to seek Him because He created you with the capability to love others the exact same way He loves us. Our part is to receive the love Our Father and Jesus have for us. Read on and you will see the proof in His Scriptures as they come to life for you personally.

Hearing from God

So many people I talk to say they never hear from Jesus. I believe they hear all the time from Jesus but they are just too busy to discern the word that they heard. Discerning the Word of God over the enemy is important. Paul wrote to the Corinthians:

1 Corinthians 14:10 There are, it may be, so many kinds of voices in the world, and none of them is without signification.

So many kinds of voices in the world and discerning the voices are up to us. Yes, every thought you have has someone's signature on it. Think about advertisements. Their signature is really obvious, you know – *buy our product*. Other thoughts are not so easy to discern. As you read the Scriptures in your Holy Bible, ask Jesus for the gifts of his understanding and His wisdom. For with these Godly gifts you will start understanding your thoughts and have His wisdom to know the origin of your thoughts. Jesus said in Genesis:

Genesis 3:11 And he said, Who told thee that thou wast naked? Hast thou eaten of the tree, whereof I commanded thee that thou shouldest not eat?

Right in Genesis we see discernment on display as Jesus asks Adam. *Who told thee that thou wast naked?* Jesus in His word talks about discernment. Discernment comes from having the Holy Spirit in our heart. But what if you haven't asked the Holy Spirit into your heart yet? Don't worry, there is still time and Jesus is still waiting for His invitation.

Remember that God will not leave you or forsake you. God is our teacher and His class room is our world. We live in His class room. The job of us believers is to be an example of his love. God Himself will put a believer in your path who will give you the desire to know God and this believer will introduce you to the Holy Spirit.

For an example, how did you find out you liked ice cream? Someone probably treated you one before. How did you find out there might be a better way of life? You find out because someone displayed a better way of living to you. In the Scriptures, we believers are likened too farmers planting seeds. We just plant the seed of God's sweet love but God transforms the seed in to a believer. With ice cream, you will have to earn enough money to buy yourself another treat. You will find as you read on that the sweet love of God has already been paid for and with discernment you will see you cannot earn the sweet love of Jesus. His sweet love is a gift we cannot earn, but we will become.

The best discerning tool we have is Jesus Himself. Read about the life of Jesus to become His life. Jesus said that He only did what He saw His Father do. So we should only do what we see Jesus do and we will only know what Jesus did by reading His life. The life of Jesus is recorded for us in His Holy Bible so Jesus is our discerning tool. By only doing what His Father did Jesus became God like. We only do what Jesus did and we will become God like also. We know what Jesus did by reading about His life in His Holy Bible.

Here is an example of a simple discernment tool: as you read the life of Jesus, you will see Jesus forgives everyone. Therefore, any voice that tells you to hold unforgiveness toward someone is not from God. If you listen to the voice that is telling you the problem is just too grievous to forgive, then you are listening to the devil. Now listen to the other voice in your head that is telling you to forgive – that is the voice of God talking to you. Jesus will always tell you to forgive and Jesus will help you forgive. To discern the voice of Jesus, simply ask Him how to forgive and you will hear His voice.

Here is another simple discernment tool from my Jesus. While here on Earth, Jesus never condemned anyone and Jesus never condoned sin. So if you have ever had a thought like '*I hope they go*

9

to hell then that thought is clearly not of God. Discern that voice telling you to condemn someone to hell. For Jesus never condemned anyone. I believe we are to hate the sin but love the sinner. Listen to what Jesus told the lady who was caught in adultery that according to the Law of Moses or the Jewish interpolation of the law was to be stoned to death. Notice in the Scriptures Jesus is referred to as a teacher because He is. Listen to the gentle kindness of my Jesus. Listen to His heart.

John 8:4-12 They said to Him, "Teacher, this woman was caught in adultery, in the very act. Now Moses, in the law, commanded us that such should be stoned. But what do You say?" This they said, testing Him, that they might have something of which to accuse Him. But Jesus stooped down and wrote on the ground with His finger, as though He did not hear. So when they continued asking Him, He raised Himself up and said to them, "He who is without sin among you, let him throw a stone at her first." And again He stooped down and wrote on the ground. Then those who heard it, being convicted by their conscience, went out one by one, beginning with the oldest even to the last. And Jesus was left alone, and the woman standing in the midst. When Jesus had lifted up himself, and saw none but the woman, he said unto her, Woman, where are those thine accusers? hath no man condemned thee? She said, No man, Lord. And Jesus said unto her, Neither do I condemn thee: go, and sin no more. Then spake Jesus again unto them, saying, I am the light of the world: he that followeth me shall not walk in darkness, but shall have the light of life.

Jesus told the woman neither do I condemn thee: go and sin no more. I believe Jesus gave her freedom, forgiveness, love and life. The woman in the story of John you just read was a prostitute. A man or a woman living the lifestyle of prostitution is really looking for love, even if the love he or she is receiving is momentary. Jesus gave her His loving forgiveness but for her to receive His loving forgiveness she needed to believe that she was forgiven – she needed to believe her past is forgiven. So Jesus told her *'neither do I condemn thee, go and sin no more.'* I believe we all have a past we are not to proud of and I believe Jesus is just waiting for you to get quiet so He can say to you *'neither do I condemn thee, go and sin no more'* and receive my love so you will stop stoning yourself.

I wish I could have been there to see the love in His eyes for I believe Jesus was talking heart to heart and eye to eye. The heart of Jesus said believe you are forgiven and believe you are loved by the son of God; for when you believe in my love, you will receive my love and the loving forgiveness of my Father. I know this is true for it is written the Son of God can do nothing of Himself but what He sees the Father do. Jesus gave her the same commission He has given us – now go live in my love and my Father's love and don't live in the sin of unbelief anymore.

Her sin of prostitution was really a sin of unbelief and I am pretty sure she knows the penalty for her sin. She lived under the Law of Moses that called for her to be stoned to death and yet her need to feel love overcame her fear of the law and death. I believe we all have the same desire to be loved and almost all of us have sin a similar sin today. I believe we have all heard the voice of the devil telling us to ignore the morals of God's Word and go sin because everyone is doing it. It seems permission for that life style is on television, internet, and everywhere except in God's Word.

Her past had brought her into the sin of unbelief. She probably never walked in the love of knowing Jesus. The day Jesus came in to her life was when His truth came into her life. His truth tells us by faith we are loved and His forgiveness is real. The real love of Jesus and real relationship with Jesus will totally remove the desire for momentary needs. I am forgiven and pray you come to know the forgiveness of my Jesus also. My future is bright. I live in the light, my eyes do shine, and my heart is glowing because my heart knows my walk is His love showing, growing and glowing. You won't find this anywhere except in your quiet time with my Jesus.

I want to show you another discernment tool in this story. If the adulterous woman got caught in the very act of adultery today, there are churches she could go to and receive what I call religious forgiveness. It is a counter fit of God's forgiveness. Religious forgiveness sounds like this: "Oh you poor thing, if your husband was a better lover you wouldn't need to go outside your marriage to find love. Those righteous hypocrite men should stone themselves. Girl, you are better then this. I would like to get your husband in here and tell him a thing or two. This is his fault and you are a victim. Listen girl, you go home with your head held high and if your loser husband says anything to you, give him a piece of your mind."

Doesn't sound like Jesus at all, does it? Yet she feels better, she feels forgiven and she didn't have to take responsibility for her action. Transferring the blame is a trick of the devil. The forgiveness of Jesus allowed the girl in John 8 to take responsibility for her action, (*go and sin no more*) and the forgiveness of Jesus brought her peace (*not go spread the blame and go tell your husband off*) and the forgiveness of Jesus gave her a new focus (*seek ye first the kingdom of God and His righteousness*) and the forgiveness of Jesus gave her hope and a better way of life (*you are worthy of my love if you simply repent and believe you are forgiven*). Yes, the knowledge of God in us – that we are made in His image and likeness and with the help of Holy Spirit we will simply overtake the flesh in us and brighten our future if we believe in His love for us and though our belief we know all things are possible.

Jesus said, "I am the light of the world, he that followeth me shall not walk in darkness, but shall have the light of life." As you read your Holy Bible, you will recognize sin is darkness and death. But light is His forgiveness. His goodness and His love are shining through you to a life everlasting. With the Holy Spirit in you and with faith in God being your source of discernment, then the WHO is talking to you will become as recognizable as His light is to darkness. Please pray for the people in religion to come into the light of discerning God's Holy Word so they too can be a giver of His light.

To believe you cannot discern the voice of Jesus is like believing you cannot be loved. I mean, Jesus came to live the Father's love to us and Jesus showed us how important talking, listening and fellowshipping is to Him and His Father. I pray this book is giving you a desire to know and trust in the love of my Jesus.

If you love someone you will want to talk to them and not just read about them. You will want to be with them. You will want to spend time with them and you will want them to be intimately connected to you through trust. Jesus is the same way. He desires to love on you today, Jesus desires to talk to you today and Jesus desires to spend time with you today. Jesus came to give us access to Himself 24/7. His love is available to us 24/7. Receive the love of Jesus by believing in the love of Jesus.

John 3:17 For God did not send His Son into the world to condemn the world, but that the world through Him might be saved.

Jesus came to save the world. I believe to Jesus the world is us, you and I. We are the world and we are to be saved by our belief in Jesus being the son of God.

We must make hearing our priority. I say this because Jesus makes talking to us His priority. Read and listen to Jesus speaking to this Samaritan woman.

John 4:6-14 Now Jacob's well was there. Jesus therefore, being wearied from His journey, sat thus by the well. It was about the sixth hour. A woman of Samaria came to draw water. Jesus said to her, "Give Me a drink." For His disciples had gone away into the city to buy food. Then the woman of Samaria said to Him, "How is it that You, being a Jew, ask a drink from me, a Samaritan woman?" For Jews have no dealings with Samaritans. Jesus answered and said to her, "If you knew the gift of God, and who it is who says to you, 'Give Me a drink,' you would have asked Him, and He would have given you living water." The woman said to Him, "Sir, You have nothing to draw with, and the well is deep. Where then do You get that living water? Are You greater than our father Jacob, who gave us the well, and drank from it himself, as well as his sons and his livestock?" Jesus answered and said to her, "Whoever drinks of this water will thirst again, but whoever drinks of the water that I shall give him will never thirst. But the water that I shall give him will become in him a fountain of water springing up into everlasting life."

If a stranger said these words to me, I probably would think he was deranged. I would think this is not the way we talk today to bring someone into the knowledge of God.

John 4:15-29 The woman said to Him, "Sir, give me this water, that I may not thirst, nor come here to draw." Jesus said to her, "Go, call your husband, and come here." The woman answered and said, "I have no husband." Jesus said to her, "You have well said, 'I have no husband,' for you have had five husbands, and the one whom you now have is not your husband; in that you spoke truly." The woman said to Him, "Sir, I perceive that You are a prophet. Our fathers worshiped on this mountain, and you Jews say that in Jerusalem is the place where one ought to worship." Jesus said to her, "Woman, believe Me, the hour is coming when you will neither on this mountain, nor in Jerusalem, worship the Father. You worship what you do not know; we know what we worship, for salvation is of the Jews. But the hour is coming, and now is, when the true worshipers will worship the Father in spirit and truth; for the Father is seeking such to worship Him. God is Spirit, and those who worship Him must worship in spirit and truth." The woman said to Him, "I know that Messiah is coming" (who is called Christ). "When He comes, He will tell us all things." Jesus said to her, "I who speak to you am He." And at this point His disciples came, and they marveled that He talked with a woman; yet no one said, "What do You seek?" or, "Why are You talking with her?" The woman then left her waterpot, went her way into the city, and said to the men, "Come, see a Man who told me all things that I ever did. Could this be the Christ?"

This had to bring great joy to Jesus. I mean the woman left and immediately professed her belief to the men of her town. She thinks she had met the Christ! Think about this for a minute. She had five husbands and was living with a man now. Is this the kind of woman you want running around telling people about you or being your ambassador?

I only talked about her reputation to make a point. Today in some churches we are told to clean up our act. We feel we must make ourselves worthy to be a spoke person for God. She was telling people to come see Jesus and at this point Jesus never even told her to repent. I believe Jesus knew she would repent because she believed. What I am saying is we do not repent as a means to believe. We repent because we do believe. The people of the city listened and came to hear if this man Jesus was as she said.

John 4:30-43 Then they went out of the city and came to Him. In the meantime His disciples urged Him, saying, "Rabbi, eat." But He said to them, "I have food to eat of which you do not know." Therefore the disciples said to one another, "Has anyone brought Him anything to eat?" Jesus said to them, "My food is to do the will of Him who sent Me, and to finish His work. Do you not say, 'There are still four months and then comes the harvest'? Behold, I say to you, lift up your eyes and look at the fields, for they are already white for harvest! And he who reaps

14

receives wages, and gathers fruit for eternal life, that both he who sows and he who reaps may rejoice together. For in this the saying is true: 'One sows and another reaps.' I sent you to reap that for which you have not labored; others have labored, and you have entered into their labors." And many of the Samaritans of that city believed in Him because of the word of the woman who testified, "He told me all that I ever did." So when the Samaritans had come to Him, they urged Him to stay with them; and He stayed there two days. And many more believed because of His own word. Then they said to the woman, "Now we believe, not because of what you said, for we ourselves have heard Him and we know that this is indeed the Christ, the Savior of the world." Now after the two days He departed from there and went to Galilee.

Please ask Jesus to help you understand all that was going on here. Notice when the men from town came and ask Jesus to stay. Jesus didn't say, "Well, let me check my schedule." Jesus didn't say, "Listen, I would like to stay and talk but I have this appointment to get beat beyond recognition and nailed to a cross coming up real soon and I need some time to prepare." No. Jesus made the people who were willing to listen to His priority. Jesus stayed for two days. Two days was enough for the people to listen and receive the truth. Jesus was and is the Son of God.

Notice what the people said to the woman after they heard Jesus.

John 4:42 Then they said to the woman, "Now we believe, not because of what you said, for we ourselves have heard Him and we know that this is indeed the Christ, the Savior of the world."

The Scriptures tell us the people believed. Not because of what the woman said but because they heard for themselves. This is crucial to understand. The moment she believed the woman became a messenger for the Word of Jesus Christ. She couldn't explain Him, she had not studied for years, but her excitement and new found joy overflowed to the village she went too. She gave the people of her village the desire to know who Jesus Christ is. My desire in writing this book is likened to that of the woman. I have a desire to share what God is doing in my life. I am hoping by doing so your desire will be on fire! For I know Jesus will stay and talk to you also.

We have the same message. We are to give people the desire to know God intimately. We are to tell people where Jesus is speaking today – in our heart. We are to help them find a quiet place to listen and we are to let them know the Holy Spirit of God will never leave you or forsake you.

Jesus is still longing for us to invite Him into our heart and Jesus desires for us to meet Him. You invite Jesus in by seeking the kingdom of God and His righteous and making Him your priority over the things of this world.

Try to imagine being God and sending your Son Jesus to Earth again. This time, everyone knows He is Jesus – the Son of God. I mean, Jesus comes in a supernatural way so there is just no doubt. Let us imagine Jesus is making a tour of America and all the preachers in all the churches in your area announce Jesus is coming Friday night and Jesus is speaking in your town.

Friday comes and less then ten percent of the congregations show up. On Sunday the preachers ask the congregations where are they last Friday and the people say, "Preacher, you know Friday night our favorite television show is on and we didn't want to miss it. Jesus should come on Saturday night instead." My point is it seems to me we are all to busy to talk to God and if we are too busy to talk to God when we have access 24/7 when will the time be right? We don't even have to go to the well to meet Him for He comes to us. Jesus is perfectly in love with us and Jesus wants us to be His messengers.

Can you imagine telling someone you love them but every time she tries to talk to you, you say "Wait until this television show is over," or "I'm on the internet now so call me later," or "I'm in church singing about how much I love you Jesus so come back later." If your heart puts preference on television or the internet or sports or whatever, then believe me that you are missing the best of God. I simply must ask everyone again, if we are too busy to hear from God when we have access 24/7 then WHEN will the time be right?

When I met my wife Jenny I had a desire to know her better. If Jenny would have said, "Ron, if you want to go out with me you must stop watching television, turn off the internet, stop watching sports, stop smoking, stop drinking, stop, stop, stop." I don't think I would have wanted to date her. I thank God Jenny was not demanding.

After I dated Jenny awhile we fall in love and we married. After a couple years of marriage, I realized I made time to watch television my priority. On some occasions I've told Jenny that I will talk to her after the show is over. One day I noticed the hurt look in her eyes when I told her that I'll talk to her after my show is over. I know now it was God who let me see the hurt look in Jenny's eyes and I thank God for letting me see the hurt in her eyes. I didn't even think about the priority I was setting but Jenny knew she was second place to the television.

Jenny could've gotten angry and stood in front of the television or unplugged it to get my attention. But thank you, Jesus for Jenny had a relationship with You and she let Jesus handle me. Jesus gave me a love for my Jenny that I didn't want to hurt her. When I saw my Jenny hurting something inside of me started hurting and I thank you Jesus I didn't ignore the hurt.

I believe the love of Jesus is the same way. Jesus will not send a lighting blot down and blow up your television to get your attention. I believe Jesus will put a believer in your life to be an example of His love to you. What you do with His love is a choice only you can make. I believe when I saw the hurt in Jenny's eyes I was really seeing the hurt in the eyes of my Jesus. I thank God one look was enough.

Discerning distractions is really easy. If your distraction takes you away form God's voice then get rid of your distractions. You have to make hearing His voice a priority in your life. Turn off the distractions. Jesus in His word said, "I will never leave you or forsake you" but I believe He will get quiet if we are too busy to listen. I hear from God the best when God is telling me what to write in the books He has given me to write, such as this book. You too will hear from God when you set some time to listen. Remember that God is available 24/7 so the time is right and that is *right now!* Seek ye first the kingdom of God and His righteousness and you will be joyful the rest of your life and you will not miss the things of this world.

I remember when I read in Genesis about Jesus coming in the cool of the day.

Genesis 3:8 And they heard the voice of the LORD God walking in the garden in the cool of the day: and Adam and his wife hid themselves from the presence of the LORD God amongst the trees of the garden.

When I read Genesis 3:8, I put my Holy Bible down and starts asking God to come to me and talk to me in the cool of the day. At first, I thought the cool of the day was the evening. In a short time I found waiting until I was quiet in the evening did not work to good for me. I would be too tired or still busy, still trying to finish the day's work. So working and family things always seemed to get in the way of my time with Jesus, but somehow I always seemed to have time to watch television.

As time passed, I felt prompted to have my quiet time in the morning. This works the best for me. I was fresh in the morning. And I found out when I dedicated my day to Jesus and to what He needed done that day, I would have a great day. Yes, making Jesus my first priority has made for a great day, a great week and lots of great years.

Please give your time to Jesus by dying to yourself and seeking Him first. You will learn in short order Jesus has the coolest personality. Jesus will turn your life into good times with Jesus. I would like to say at my starting point, which was many years ago, in my walk with Jesus that I didn't give God any thanks for His prompting me to have our quiet time in the morning. I actually though it was just me changing my own priorities. Now through the discernment Jesus has given me, I recognize the prompting to have quiet time in the morning is from God and now I have given Him the credit and will give Him the credit for I have come to know without God I cannot breath.

Jesus has a cool personality.

Okay, I can hear you're asking. You want a story about the cool personality of Jesus?

Last fall I was in Colorado Springs camping. I knew Andrew Womack was building a new school up on a mountain somewhere around there. After inquiring, I started my way to the school on a

Friday afternoon. On the way, I just voiced out loud in my car, "Jesus I would like to meet Berry Bennett." Berry is a teacher at the school and I had a DVD of his and I liked the way he teaches. I liked listening to him and I thought I would like to meet him.

At the college I was greeted by a young girl who asks me if I was there for a tour. I didn't realize they do tours of the school but I agree that I would love to go on a tour. She informed me the last tour for the day was over but I could come back Monday and go on one. I mentioned to her that I live in a camper and was planning on leaving the area Monday morning. She smiled and said, "I am finished here so let me lock the door and I will take you on a tour."

We went through the whole first floor. And as we started down the hallway to the elevator, I saw a huge men's room. I really need to use the men's room but I thought I am taking up so much of this young girl's time so I think I can hold off. When we came out of the elevator on the lower level I saw another men's room. I asked her if she wouldn't mind and she replied, "Go ahead, and take your time." When I walked into the bathroom I saw Berry standing using the urinal. I started laughing out loud. He looked surprised and asked, "What's so funny?" I explained what God had done and we both laughed.

That's my Jesus and it is for sure no one could love me more.

As you learn God's Word you will come to know God loves to see us put our faith in Him. Here in this chapter we are talking about hearing from God and I want to say I hear from God by faith and I have come to recognize faith comes from hearing God.

Romans 10:17 So faith comes from hearing, and hearing through the word of Christ.

I believe as we read the Word of God we will recognize His Word as truth and truth brings peace into our heart. Peace allows us to relax and as we relax we will hear well. The better we hear, the more we believe and belief allows Jesus to transform our belief into faith. Faith is an action word. Have you ever fallen in love? If you have been in love, could you keep your love a secret? Could you hide your love around your friends? God knows love shows.

I mean the love of God shows. His love grows and His love knows. Love shows by your actions towards each other, love never stops growing because you always want to meet the needs of the one you love every day. Love knows because if you love someone you will prove your love by being attentive and listening to your loved one all the time. When you are listening and being attentive to the needs of your loved one you will build their faith in you to always be there for them. Faith and love are discerning tools.

I believe here in America, someone is telling us to turn off our love for each other. Who do you think is telling us to turn off our love? Who tells us to focus our eyes on everything but people? Have you ever noticed how people like to go to coffee shops to be around people? It seems people don't like to be alone yet they don't want to be bothered with people face to face. These people bring their computers to a coffee shop and stare at it for hours. These people like to text better then talking. I think people have an inherent need to be social but we have reduced this need to just being around others and not allowing others to get in our heart.

The first time I experienced this cold-heartedness was when I was in Vietnam. Being cold-hearted is a self protection tool. In Vietnam, no one wanted to get to know you because there was a good chance you were going to be killed. If the people around you didn't know you, then when you died you become just a number inside a body bag. It is a lot easier to look at a number rather than a face. I was saddened by the heartlessness in my comrades in Vietnam and because I didn't know what to do about it, I became like them.

Now I am saddened by what I see in coffee shops today in stores and in the world. But today, I have hope and my heart is glad and by faith in God and having relationship with Jesus means I can do something about the sadness in others. The good news is Jesus came and gave us His heart of love and if we believe we can have His heart of love in us. We become His love to others. I have faith in His love being in me and His love is transforming the world one heart at a time. Now because I know Jesus, I have hope for my neighbor, I have love for my city, and I know my country and my world will be transformed by the love of Jesus.

Having quiet time with Jesus is a joy beyond our understanding. In my quiet time, God teaches me and He gives me wisdom and my faith grows. Through faith in God, my hope for this world grows. We all have the ability to listen. And Jesus said, "My sheep know my voice and my sheep will follow me all the way to victory."

Jesus speaks to me in my heart. But when God wants me to do something I simply feel a prompting to do it. I believe God gives me prompting because to act on a prompting is living out my faith. So doing what God is prompting us to do is the works of faith that God talks about in His Holy Bible. I live in a camper and travel all the time. People ask me how I know where to go, if I pray and ask God where to go. I tell them that I never pray about where I go because I just know by faith that if I am going the wrong way, then my God will turn me around.

My walk with my Lord brings so much joy into my heart that to miss a day of talking to God is really hard for me. It is like missing my Jenny. Yes, missing Jesus for a day is missing the love of my life. I have a sadness that comes to my heart when I become too busy to talk to my Jesus. I mean, I hear from Jesus 24/7 but I can still miss Him.

My Jenny and I could be together and even in the same room while being around friends. Yet, after a couple hours of socializing we would miss each other and we looked forward to when the event will be over so we could talk together without the distractions of the world. My relationship with Jesus is the same way. I can even be in church and talk to everyone there about Jesus, but in my heart I am still missing my personal time with my Jesus.

In my younger years, I would hear people say "I heard from God or God revealed this to me," and I thought, "Why do I not hear from you, Lord?" In the back of my mind, I thought those people must be really special to hear from God. I continued to read my Holy Bible and I ask questions to everyone whom I thought knew more of the Lord than I. I didn't realize then that God was teaching me discernment and I hadn't really realized God would talk to me. This seemed so hard to believe at first that God, the creator of the universe would talk to me.

My break through started really happened when I went right to my Jesus and ask God my questions instead of asking friends and people I thought know God. I would read a passage or a Scripture and ask God, "Jesus what are you teaching me in this scripture?" And before long, I would receive understanding. Remember in John 14:26:

John 14:26 But the Comforter, which is the Holy Ghost, whom the Father will send in my name, he shall teach you all things, and bring all things to your remembrance, whatsoever I have said unto you.

Yes, Jesus said "He would bring all things to your remembrance, whatsoever I have said unto you." We simply must set some quiet time a side to hear from Jesus. Remember that Jesus said whatsoever I have said unto you, I will bring back to your remembrance, not the words others have said to us but His Words, he will bring to our remembrance. We must simply set some time aside to listen to Jesus, the Word made flesh. To hear from God and to know that we are hearing from God takes faith that God wants to talk to us. You receive His faith when we spend quiet time reading His word and listening for HIS VOICE to tell us the meaning of what we have heard.

I want to share for a moment. When I first sit down and listened quietly for His voice, I was unsuccessful. So I turned off all the distractions. I got up real early in the morning while Jenny was still sleeping. I tried really hard to listen but the jokes I told years ago came into my mind. I said out loud, "Jesus, why am I thinking about dirty jokes I used to tell?" My mind would drift and I just started to give up. Thank you, Jesus that I didn't give up! The Scripture, my sheep know my voice kept coming into my mind and I cried out to God why can't I hear you. Finally, after months of trying I heard from God, Jesus told me to write a book about my Jenny. I said, "Okay, but you have to help me Jesus."

That day, I opened my computer and turned on word. Within no time, the first book was finished. I had started hearing from God everyday and we have the coolest conversations. I don't know if this had something to do with why it took so long for me to hear from God but God had told me to write a book about Jenny a couple years earlier and I was too busy.

God has lots of ways for us to hear Him. Here is a funny story that happened a few days ago. While I was talking with a friend who has a six-year old boy and a four-year old girl, she brought some coloring books to the table to keep her children occupied. As we talked, she started coloring. When I ask her why, she simply said that she can listen better when her hands are occupied.

As we went on talking, I suddenly remembered a study some teachers did years ago that proved children can listen better when their hands were occupied with a simple task. The next day in my Coffee Time With Jesus, I ask Jesus if this were true? Jesus answered, saying "Why do you think I tell you to wax your camper?" I started laughing and said, "So we can talk all day without me getting fidgety." I think I could hear Jesus laughing as He said, "That's right!" Jesus brings so much joy to my life.

I believe Jesus tells me to write these books because I have my mind set on Him the whole time I am writing. My eyes are following what He tells me though His books and my heart receives His truths. More good news for me is by writing these books I have to read them over and over, so his truths go into my heart over and over.

Discernment

Please don't let circumstances dictate your walk with the Lord. If we go by circumstances, the circumstance we are in will dictate our life, our love and our joy. You might be thinking right now how circumstances can dictate our lives. For an example, if the bills are paid then God is good and we think He must love us and we are happy. But let something go wrong and we ask "God, why did that happen?" or "Where are you Lord?" or worse yet we ask, "Do you love me Lord?"

Not knowing we are loved is the source of all those questions. Without a personal relationship with God, our life will be full of ups and downs – happy one minute and sad the next. We need understanding of the perfect love God has for us. For without knowledge of His love we will let the circumstances dictate our life and we will try to find happiness by becoming materialistic. That is we will evaluate our life on momentary happiness and what we have in our position instead of His everlasting love for us. We will let the world dictate to us our worth instead of what God says we are worth.

Jesus will take the ups and downs out of our life according to our faith in His word. To have faith, we need to discern the voices we are hearing all day long. Again, look to Jesus for the answer as to who you are listening to and look to the Word of Jesus to help you understand His truth.

Do you think Jesus could have gone through the last three days of His life without discernment? With discernment, Jesus knew His Father loved Him no matter what the circumstances were. Jesus never doubted His Fathers love. When we come into an awareness of the love God has for us we will see trials – *our cross* as a way to bring glory to God and show the world His love for us by simply believing – *while we are in the trial,* that we are loved by God.

24

All through the life of Jesus we see faith. Without faith, Jesus would not have known His Father still loved Him when He was in His trial. Without discernment we have no faith. Ask God for the spirit of discernment. You will receive the Holy Spirit of discernment and you will become who you are listening too.

Here is an example of living without discernment. Hitler became who he was listening to and Hitler's life proved he lived without discernment. Contrast Hitler's life of no discernment to the life of Jesus who had discernment and the life of Jesus is the greatest example of WHO we can be if we ask Jesus into our life and ask Jesus for His spirit of discernment. Discernment is a free gift from God! To get your free gift of discernment from God all you need to do is believe He will give you His free gift of discernment.

Discernment is very important so please read in your Holy Bible about the life of Jesus. Read to live His life and to become the life of Jesus. Please do not read to know Jesus, but read to become Jesus, read to become so close to Jesus the two of you are one. Yes through discernment we will see Jesus as our source of knowledge, our source of truth, our source of life and our source of discernment. Jesus is my Protector, my Provider and my source of discernment. Sometimes I need extra help discerning so I go right to my Jesus and ask Him to back up what I am hearing with Scripture and Jesus will lead me right into a Scripture that makes what I am hearing perfectly clear.

Through discernment, Jesus has come to live with me. I have my trust in Him, I have my faith in Him, I have freedom from fear in Him and I don't want to live a day without Him. Please start your day by asking Jesus for the relationship He came and died to give us. Don't just sing to Him on Sunday morning. Please ask Jesus to let you become Him. Jesus said seek Him and you will find Him.

Jesus is not some distant person off in heaven somewhere. Jesus said we can have His eyes, His heart, His mind, and Jesus said He made us in His image and likeness. Jesus made us His way so we can become His representative here on Earth if we desire to be. Thank you God we have the freedom to choose! Choose the devil and manifest hate like Hitler did. Or choose Jesus and manifest His loving forgiveness to everyone.

We must simply ask Jesus into our heart, into our life and then we can become His loving forgiveness to all, we will have His mind, His eyes, and His heart of love to share with everyone we meet. Our precious walk with the Lord is joy beyond our understanding. By asking Jesus for this precious walk with Him and by setting time a side to hear from Him, we will become one with Him just like He was one with the Father when He walked this earth. Remember all things are possible to those who know they are loved by God and to those who choose to live as His loving ambassador. Remember we can become His thoughts. We can speak His words because we hear His voice, and we see people with compassion and we become His image and likeness. Pray today to become His image and likeness today.

Do our earthly accomplishments please God?

I would like to share one more thought about the important stuff that could take us away from hearing the voice of God. Paul writes in Philippians about what he thought were his great accomplishments and how he thought his great accomplishments would please God.

Philippians 3:6   When it comes to being enthusiastic, I was a persecutor of the church. When it comes to winning God's approval by keeping Jewish laws, I was perfect.

These were Saul's accomplishments. Now listen to the transformed Saul to Paul accomplishments. This is some good discernment.

Philippians 3:7-9 These things that I once considered valuable, I now consider worthless for Christ. It's far more than that! I consider everything else worthless because I'm much better off knowing Christ Jesus my Lord. It's because of him that I think of everything as worthless. I threw it all away in order to gain Christ and to have a relationship with him. This means that I didn't receive God's approval by obeying his laws. The opposite is true! I have God's approval through faith in Christ. This is the approval that comes from God and is based on faith

In Philippians 3:7 Paul says the things he once considered valuable – his accomplishments, now he considers them worthless compared to a life of knowing Jesus Christ. The things Paul once put great value on, he now sees as worthless compared to knowing my Jesus. Paul goes on to say compared to the knowledge of knowing Jesus Christ, "I consider everything else worthless" that is all the things of this world are considered worthless "because I'm much better off knowing Christ Jesus my Lord." I believe now is the time to ask Jesus to be your best friend but remember I am His favorite.

In the King James Version, Paul calls the things of this world *'dung.'* I believe Paul has rightly judged the things of this world or the distractions of this world by calling them worthless and dung. What will you choose: worthless dung – the accomplishments of this world or a life of peace, joy, and loving others? Personally, I choose to know Jesus is my personal Savior. I think this is one of the greatest revelations Jesus has ever given me. I will never again spend one moment working for dung when I can use my time to be an example of God's love.

The amazing thing about the world today is people will spend their entire life working to build up a pile of dung. We have insurance to replace our dung if something happens to it. We even take out mortgages to get the dung today as if having dung is so important. Then we read in His Word that Jesus doesn't like us having two masters. Yes, debt is a master over us and yet we pray and ask God to help us get loans for dung and then ask God to help us get out of our dung debt. As stupid as that sounds is, I believe it is true for most of us and on top of all that Jesus still loves us and Jesus will make us His best friends if we let Him.

Luke 16:13-14 "No servant can serve two masters, for either he will hate the one and love the other, or he will be devoted to the one and despise the other. You cannot serve God and money." The Pharisees, who were lovers of money, heard all these things, and they ridiculed him.

The Pharisees seemed to have *no* discernment.

I have a lot of people tell me I am wrong on this one. They tell me that to live in the world today we almost have to be in debt.

I wonder as they ridicule me if they have any faith at all. I have to admit too I lived with a mortgage payment until 2002. I figured I would either be paying a mortgage that would end be paid off or paying rent that would never end. I thank God for showing me an end to those thoughts and bring me into a faith that my God will take care of me. Now I live in peace, hope, and the loving joy of the Lord instead of dreading the end of the month mortgage payment.

A couple years ago, Jesus and I wrote a story called *Your Inheritance* and it is in the *Joy of the Lord* book. In this story, I called the things of this world as material stuff. When Jesus and I were almost finished writing, Jesus told me one morning in our Coffee Time With Jesus that I need to change the words material stuff to the word *junk* in that story. I did and I believe Jesus sees all the material stuff here on earth as junk. Jesus tells us in Matthew 6:19-21:

Matthew 6:19-21 Do not lay up for yourselves treasures on earth, where moth and rust destroy and where thieves break in and steal, but lay up for yourselves treasures in heaven, where neither moth nor rust destroys and where thieves do not break in and steal. For where your treasure is, there your heart will be also.

As we read the Words of Jesus, we must hear the heart of Jesus. For where your treasure is there your heart will be also. I want my heart of Jesus all the time and I believe Jesus has gently removed my desire to have earthly junk. I thank you Jesus for your love for me and desiring to be with me so much. You have given me my greatest joy and that is spending time with you.

Paul says he would throw all the things of the world away in order to gain Jesus Christ and to have relationship with Jesus. Then Paul said he didn't receive the approval of God by obeying His laws. In fact the opposite is true. Paul received approval of God by having faith in Jesus Christ. We too can please Jesus by our simple faith in Jesus.

We read earlier how the apostles pleased God by faith. In my Holy Bible, Jesus tells me without faith I cannot please Him. I believed Jesus showed us by doing healings on the Sabbath. He would rather see works of faith done seven days a week then to let His children suffer because we want to keep the law. I believe Paul realized by having His faith in Jesus he could not break the law.

Personally I will honor the Sabbath by going to church and telling testimonies of what God has done this week. But I will heal the sick and raise the dead and cast out devils on the Sabbath also. I will love my Lord with my whole heart and mind and soul on the Sabbath and I will honor my Jesus by being His ambassador seven days a week. I will love my neighbor as myself and keep the commandments and I will do these things through faith. And I will by faith please my Jesus, my Father God and their Holy Spirit living in me will jump for joy. Living and knowing I am His favorite means I will go to heaven with a list of Jesus accomplishments.

Is our focus on the past or the future?

We all know how Saul was a terrible person in his early years. I wonder if Saul had a mother praying for him. I thank God for transforming him into a son of God. The only way Paul kept his transformation was by faith. If Paul didn't believe in the forgiveness of God and the love Jesus showed him, then Paul would have never been the great man of faith he was transformed into.

I want to bring attention to what Paul focused on once he was transformed. The moment Paul was transformed by Jesus; Paul looked to what Jesus had for him to do. Paul simply made himself available to Jesus and then never looked back to his past life. Paul never let his past stop Him from doing what God had for Him to do today.

How can we ever have a precious walk with my Jesus if we are focused on the past or what the devil is doing? Nowhere in the Holy Bible are we told to dwell on the past. When I hear of people looking to their past, studying there past, trying to peel off another layer of some imaginary onion – I mean do they believe Jesus already died for our sins, to set free, to open us to personal commutation, to show us a perfect walk or not?

Listen to words Jesus spoke at the well.

John 4:16-18 Jesus said to her, "Go, call your husband, and come here." The woman answered him, "I have no husband." Jesus said to her, "You are right in saying, 'I have no husband'; for you have had five husbands, and the one you now have is not your husband. What you have said is true."

Notice Jesus didn't condemn her for having five husbands. Jesus praised her for telling Him the truth. Jesus didn't ask her about the details of her life. Jesus didn't tell her to go some place for a couple years and dig up your past and beg me forgiveness for each detail. Jesus never did the religious things we tell people today. The story goes on to say the woman got saved and the whole town got saved. In a split second that woman received the loving forgiveness of God and ran to town to tell everyone, "Come see the man who told me everything ever I did."

Religious people today will tell you to dig up your past and try real hard to repent for every detail. At one ministry I went to, I was even told to ask the Holy Spirit to help me dig up my past and ask the Holy Spirit to show the curses handed down. Talk about digging yourself into a hole of no return! I even got mad at the Holy Spirit for not revealing the sin I thought I must be in. I thought the Holy Spirit was holding back Jenny's healing. I believed the people at that ministry almost lost relationship with God because of listening to man's wisdom – *religion* instead of seeking first the kingdom of God. Jesus is truth and mans wisdom is a hole of no return.

I mentioned this because I want to make as clear as possible that we have one teacher – Jesus Christ. We are to follow Him and not the religions of men. We are to seek ye first the kingdom of God and His righteousness by reading His Word and asking Jesus to reveal His truth to us. If you are struggling with your past, please ask the Holy Spirit for discernment and believe you will be free and YOU WILL BE FREE because my Jesus said so, not the doctrine of man.

Look at what Jesus did at the well. Look at the results. People read the Word, believe the Word, live the Word, and enjoy heaven on earth now! Jesus is heaven on earth now. And if there is a bus coming, it should be overcrowded because of the seeds of love you have sown through Jesus. This life is not about getting your own seat on the bus. This life is about filling the bus for Jesus and don't worry about the bus being overcrowded because there might be a limousine coming for you.

John 4:28-30 So the woman left her water jar and went away into town and said to the people, "Come, see a man who told me all that I ever did. Can this be the Christ?" They went out of the town and were coming to him.

I pray for the people who are dwelling on the past and mislead by looking to there past to be enlightened by the Holy Spirit to seek ye first the kingdom of God and for them to be drawn into the loving forgiveness of God. I pray for this freedom from the past to be theirs because as long as the devil keeps them in bondage to their past, they will never feel worthy of being loved and blessed by God. The woman at the well did not dwell on her past, she did not dwell on her worthiness to be forgiven and she simply heard the word of God and ran to town to tell everyone. Jesus said to love ourselves because we are made in His image and likeness. The woman at the well didn't wait for Jesus to even explain forgiveness or for Jesus to say your sins are forgiven. She just knew and believed she was forgiven and ran to tell everyone.

I wonder how God transforms anyone who is not seeking Him. Please put your focus on Jesus and His love for you. If you focus on your past you will not hear His voice, and you will not receive His love. When I sin I simply thank Jesus for His forgiveness and then I ask Him to help me sin no more. Then I get on with whatever Jesus has for me to do that day. I thank you Jesus for giving me a future with you in my heart and I thank you Jesus for forgiving my past completely. Yes I thank my Jesus I am in His new covenant.

I know I have a past. I know I am not proud of some of my past but Jesus has brought me out of the past and has showed me how to live for Him by faith and Jesus has given me a future. Jesus is no respecter of persons which means what Jesus did for Paul and the woman at the well and everyone who will listen, Jesus will do for all. I am one of the all Jesus came for and so are you. The sooner you put down the past the sooner you will be available to Jesus and His joyful future. I believe the Joy of the Lord is in hearing His voice, knowing His will and knowing you are adopted into His family. I believe this by Faith and by faith I will hear His voice daily.

Jesus, the Good Shepherd

Listen to the words of Jesus as Jesus tells us He is our Protector, Savior, Provider, Lover, and Transformer. Here Jesus refers to himself as a Good Shepherd.

John 10:14 I am the good shepherd. I know my own and my own know me

Here Jesus describes who He is the good shepherd and Jesus tells us who will be known of God. Jesus knows me and I know He knows me. Matthew 7:21-23 is a verse where someone is standing before Jesus for judgment and says, "I have cast out devils in your name and healed the sick in your name and raised the dead in your name and Jesus says depart from me I don't know you."

Matthew 7:21-23 "Not everyone who says to me, 'Lord, Lord,' will enter the kingdom of heaven, but the one who does the will of my Father who is in heaven. On that day many will say to me, 'Lord, Lord, did we not prophesy in your name, and cast out demons in your name, and do many mighty works in your name?' And then will I declare to them, 'I never knew you; depart from me, you workers of lawlessness '

I believe Jesus tells them to depart from Him for He never knew them because they never lay down their life to serve Him. They never gave their time to know the will of our Father. They never had personal time with Jesus. They just wanted the gifts to flow through them. Jesus said in John 10:15 "I lay down my life for my sheep." Just doing miracles is not enough. We must be willing to lay down our life like Jesus did. Numerous times in the Bible we are told Jesus went to have quiet time with our Father. Yes, quiet time is simply laying down our life for Jesus.

We simply must see Jesus and Father God as the Good Shepherd. The Good Shepherd will lay down his life for his sheep. The sheep know the voice of their Shepherd. Jesus has proved this is not cheap talk because He has already laid down His life for us. Thank you Jesus!

John 10:15 Just as the Father knows me and I know the Father; and I lay down my life for the sheep.

We can only know the Father by laying down our life for our Father. Please lay down your life by turning off the television and other distractions so you will come into the realm of His love where you personally will hear the voice and recognize the voice of our Father God and Jesus. Here we see Jesus is ready to lay down His life for us His believers and that makes my Jesus my Shepherd and the best part is I know Jesus is my Shepherd because I hear Jesus call me by name.

John 10:16 And I have other sheep that are not of this fold. I must bring them also, and they will listen to my voice. So there will be one flock, one shepherd.

Here I believe Jesus is telling us believers who hear His voice that we need to help others listen for His voice so the world will become believers. Therefore we will become one flock who hears and knows the voice of the one shepherd. The Holy Spirit is a big spirit and we are to share Him with everyone. He is not for me alone but for everyone everywhere.

Hearing the voice of God is a must. Hearing comes from faith and faith is believing. So hearing the Word of God isn't something we should try a couple times. And if God speaks we will start listening. Look at the words Jesus chose "I *must* bring them also and they *will listen* to my voice." Yes, in the end there will be one flock and one Shepherd. And we will hear His voice and have the Holy Spirit guiding us. I want everyone to say "I believe and by faith I hear, and the Holy Spirit of God is in me." Thank You Jesus!

This is off subject a little but I must ask how on earth we got so many denominations when right in John 10:16 we see the words of Jesus, *'So there will be one flock, one shepherd?'* There are so many denominations and they all what you to join their denomination. Yet we read *'So there will be one flock, one shepherd.'*

If the leadership of your denomination is asking you to join their denomination, ask them if their denomination is seeking the kingdom of God by manifesting the kingdom of God or building a denomination?

I have a friend, Jay who is 14 years old and when asked by a news reporter, "What denomination are you in?" Jay answered, "Sir there are no denominations in heaven, only truth. All that other stuff gets washed away." Seek ye first the kingdom of God and God will give you the answers.

Please read John 10:17 and you will see the reason Father God loves me.

John 10:17 For this reason the Father loves me, because I lay down my life that I may take it up again.

If you want to know what makes God joyful, what brings joy to into the heavenly realm, then read John 10:17 again. *"Because I lay down my life that I may take it up again."* This is the secret to joyfulness here on earth. Joyfulness is knowing the reason Father God loves us. You know this is the heaven on earth Jesus talks about. Simply start each day by asking God, "What are we going to do today." This question to my Jesus is saying I will lay down my life today to do whatever you put in front of me. People have asked me, "Do you believe laying down your life is as simple as giving your time to Jesus?" I answered, "Yes!"

I also believe we are to pick our life up again by doing whatever God puts in front of us to do with the time He has given us.

Please let Jesus have control of your day by giving Him the only thing we have to give Him — *our undivided time.* To give our life is easy when we believe in our heart Jesus conquered death. Yes, thank you Jesus. I hear your voice and thank you Jesus for proving to us believers there is no death.

John 10:18 No one takes it from me, but I lay it down of my own accord. I have authority to lay it down, and I have authority to take it up again. This charge I have received from my Father.

I hope anyone reading this has heard the expression *'Jesus gave us free will.'* Well, here is our free will in bold print. Jesus even tells us who gave us the right to choose. *"This charge I have received from my Father."* Yes, we receive our right to choose from the Father. The right to choose is a gift so use it wisely. Every choice we make effects our eternity.

Again, I beg you to lay down your life and your past to come into the new life Jesus Christ has for us by simply hearing His voice. Isn't it cool to think that we have the power to bring a smile on the face of our Father God and on the face of my Jesus? This is so clear to me. I simply choose to know God and desire to put a smile on His face. It seems today that most people live to make them happy. I pray they run into a believer – *namely you* today so they can have a face to face encounter with Jesus.

We can choose to live by faith and be known of God. We can hear from God and we can read our Holy Bible to be the walking, talking representatives of Jesus Christ. We have a choice to believe and live in the joy of life without fear of death or we can choose to be miserable searching our past, hoping to find some hidden sin Jesus has already paid the price for. Jesus gave us everything we need to do our job. He showed or modeled our job perfectly so we could come to know Him so intimately that we will hear Him, walk like Him and become so close to Him that we will be transformed by Him. We have the Holy Spirit of Jesus in us so we are His ambassadors and we are commissioned to build the kingdom of God.

Details:

I am blessed to know God as my personal savior and my personal best friend. I believe by faith I talk to God and He is listening. I tell people everywhere Jesus is in my life and I see Him in the details of my life. Have you ever ask God to help you plug in a plug? I have and I found when I ask Jesus to help me with the simplest jobs He does.

36

I have a little prayer that I say when I cannot find something. I simply say, "Dearest Jesus, this is important to me so I know it is important to you." Thank you Jesus for finding this for me and Jesus shows me where this is. You see, I don't ask God to find the missing whatever, I am simply stating I know by faith what I am looking for is important to God because it is important to me. And my Jesus will tell me where it is because it is important to Him also. I must tell you when I first started praying that prayer I thought I had thought it up. Years went by before my Jesus told me He gave that prayer. The corrections of Jesus are so gentle.

I talked about this prayer in a church one Sunday. After church, a woman asked me how I knew God wants to help me find something as simple as my car keys. In my heart, I asked my Jesus. And then I replied, "Jesus said that He would give us peace, joy, hope and love. If my wife Jenny could not find her car keys, she knew I would help her find them. Jenny knew this because she simply knew I loved her. You know, I didn't want Jenny frustrated, or sad, or giving up hope. So I would help her find something as simple as her car keys. When we found it, her joy, peace, and hope came back. I believe Jesus is the same way. Jesus loves me so Jesus will help me stay in peace, joy, hope and I know this because I know Jesus loves me. The Word of God says so and I believe and have faith in the truth of His Word.

I know by faith Jesus wants me to walk in his peace.

This simple prayer is a prayer of faith because I know Jesus really does care where my glasses are or my car keys are or where I left my coffee cup. All we need is faith to know Jesus is in the details and Jesus is listening.

For an example, a couple years ago I had to run a new power wire to the blower motor in my motor home. I connected the wire to the battery with an in line fuse to protect the wire in case of a short someday. The in line fuse cost $1.99 at auto zone. A couple years later I was driving and the blower motor quit. I checked the fuse which was under the hood. I found the fuse holder had gotten moist into it and corroded the connection. To fix the problem, I needed a new in line fuse holder.

I went to the people in the campground office to see if there was auto store nearby. They checked on the internet and told me there was a Napa auto store three miles from me. I went to the address and there was no Napa. After asking a couple people I found out the Napa had closed a couple years ago. Apparently, no one had updated the website.

I saw a man in town and he told me there was a hardware store about a mile away and a marina store down the street about four miles away. I went to the hardware store first. They had the in line fuse but it was not waterproof. So I went to marina and they had the exact same fuse holder as the hardware so I said I'll take one and worry about finding a waterproof one later when I am in a bigger city. The man rang up the part and said that will be $7.24. I said that they are $1.99 at the hardware store, to which he replied, "If I were you, I would go to the hardware store."

On my way back to the hardware store I started complaining to God. I asked God, "Why is this so frustrating to me? This seems like such a simple repair!" I felt like I was running around like a crazy man. Jesus answered me right away saying, "Ron, you didn't ask me for my help, did you?" I repented right there and asked Jesus to help me. And the rest of the job went totally prefect! Thank you Jesus for giving me peace and removing my frustration. I know you care about every detail in my life.

You see, I believed this fuse holder thing was so simple and I could handle the problem myself. I didn't say out loud or under my breath, "God I can handle this so Jesus just relax and take a break," but I must have thought it. You know, I think by not asking God into my situation I was basically denying myself a blessing of help from God. Again, thank you Jesus for being right there dwelling in me to pick me up when I started complaining. Thank you Jesus for being so gentle with me and thank you Jesus for loving me!

Here is one more little detail story. Years ago, before I realized God was a detail God, I was camping in a campground that had iron minerals in their water. I had never been around iron water. I knew I didn't like the smell or the taste, nor did I know iron water would turn things brown. After one month of living with iron water, my toilet had brown streaks coming around and down the bowl and I hated looking and using a toilet like that.

When Jenny and I left the campground, I found the water was great at our next stop. The way we were parked the sun would come up through our bedroom window and shine right on our ugly toilet. I had tried everything I could imagine to remove those ugly stains. Finally, one morning I was so frustrated and just said out loud to the Lord, "You know Jesus I hate my toilet and I don't have the money to buy another one, so I am asking You to get the money somewhere or please just show me how to clean this iron stuff off from my ugly toilet." Just then I heard Jesus say, "Use toothpaste." I started laughing and said, "I'm not using toothpaste on my toilet." Then I felt a gentle conviction. So I reached for the toothpaste and started cleaning the iron stuff off on my toilet. Within minutes, my toilet looked brand new.

I got so excited I started jumping as best as I could in my camper and praising God with everything that is in me. I looked at the toilet again, the sun was shining on it and it was shiny and pretty and I could not stop laughing. I knew every detail of my life was important to my Jesus. After I settled down a little, I realized how important I am to God. I sat holding my little Jenny on my lap and kept staring at her. I kept telling her over and over Jesus is alive and real and He loves us Jenny. At that point in our journey Jenny could still smile and I believe Jenny still had her sight and I believe my little Jenny could feel the excitement of knowing our Jesus is alive. I kept telling Jenny your healing is next I just know it.

I hope and pray everyone will come to the Lord with their concerns and allow Jesus to be Jesus. Please don't save Jesus for just the big things in life. Jesus wants more then anything to be in the little things so He can build your confidence in Him to keep you on His lighted path as you walk or journey through life.

The Word of God is true. God is alive today and God hears our prayers. If you are not hearing from God try listening better. Turn off the distractions. Create a quiet space in your heart to hear from Him and become attentive to the promptings you feel in your spirit. Jesus will prove Himself alive and Jesus will prove to you His love for you is real.

Remember Jesus has no problem talking. If you're not hearing the voice of God the problem is in your listening and it just might be you are not quiet enough to hear.

Jesus wants to be that personal with you too. Jesus likes us to ask Him into everything we do and every word we say. I hope you have Jenny's book called *Love Never Fails* because if you read it, you will see Jesus in every detail of your life. I tell you my Jesus is in the details. Please read about Moses or David in the Holy Bible and you will know Jesus is in the little things to build you up to the big things.

When you pray to God please don't pray the answer you want from God. Please pray knowing God has an answer and knowing God is the answer. For example, I don't pray for material dung or Jesus can you get me this or Jesus will you do this for me, Jesus you know I need this et cetera. I pray in faith by simply saying God I know you love me and all things are possible so have your way in me today.

Notice that I said I don't ask God for material needs but I do ask Jesus for spiritual wants that Jesus said we should ask for. These are the needs I am asking Jesus for. I ask for His eyes, His mind and His heart so I can be His light, His wisdom, His courage and His compassionate love to everyone I meet. Every day I thank You Jesus for your words of wisdom you will give me today. I thank Jesus for your Holy Spirit in me. I thank you Jesus for your love and your words in me so I may help others to desire to know you more. PS. I love you too, Jesus!

I have all my trust in my God. I don't even have an alarm clock in my camper. Life is simple for me. If I need to be up at a certain time I ask Jesus and He wakes me up. The gas gauge in my car is broken and it stays on empty all the time. If I need to know how much gas is in my tank I ask my Jesus and He makes the gauge work long enough for me to know how much gas I have. If the gauge doesn't move when I ask Him, I know by faith I have enough gas for the trip. Faith makes my life simple and worry free.

When I see a situation that I don't understand or I don't know what to say or do to help someone in need, I simply go to my source Jesus Christ and He gives me the understanding and the words. And if don't hear from God I simply don't say anything. I have a pretty simple life and I praise my Jesus for it.

To see God in every little detail we simply trust Father God and Jesus to direct my path. For example, for months now we, Jesus and I have been writing another book and together we had 208 pages finished. One morning I realized Jesus was changing the direction of the book and Jesus changed the title of the book. So we, Jesus and I, started over with His new direction and His new title and His new book was born.

I could have complained. I could have told God how many hours I have worked on the old book. I could have told God the book is nearly finished and I could have ask God why change it now. No. I know by faith I don't write to write. I simply hear from God or I do not write. To me Jesus is the author and when He changes the direction I simply follow.

I sometimes hear people complain if their comfort cooling breaks down and they get too hot, or if we complain about a flat tire or whatever. Please don't use your faith in God expecting God to give you a better day or a perfect day everyday. Instead use your faith to give someone else a perfect day. Jesus did this everyday of His life. Jesus came to give us spiritual gifts of His love and He opened up our communication with Him. Now, we are hearing from God to give someone a better day, every day.

Can you image Jesus crying to His Father, "Father, I'm tired of walking. I told you I wanted to come to Earth when the automobile was here," or "Father, why nails? Couldn't they just tie me to the cross?" Can you imagine Jesus complaining saying, "Father they just ripped my beard off my face; I mean really, really, really I mean wasn't the crown of thorns enough and oh yeah, I thought you were going to take my pain? I mean really, really."

Jesus never used His relationship with the Father to give Himself a better day. The faith of Jesus was tested over and over. I pray my faith will be tested over and over and like Jesus I pray I will shine the light of God's love through my trials by never wavering and never doubting His love for me. I pray for Jesus to be in my details and I pray for strength to forgive the men nailing me to the cross. For me, these are the sweetest details I or anyone could pray for.

This might sound stupid but I do pray for Jesus to strengthen me for my cross. I hear people pray for blessings of money. But I believe more than any of those earthly dung blessings, I pray to be blessed with a trial that brings glory to my Jesus and my Father. I pray to be strengthened in His love.

Ephesians 3:16-19 that according to the riches of his glory he may grant you to be strengthened with power through his Spirit in your inner being, so that Christ may dwell in your hearts through faith—that you, being rooted and grounded in love, may have strength to comprehend with all the saints what is the breadth and length and height and depth, and to know the love of Christ that surpasses knowledge, that you may be filled with all the fullness of God.

Here again we see the goal of Jesus. Jesus wants us to know the love of Christ that surpasses knowledge, that you may be filled with all the fullness of God. I am so blessed to receive this Scripture in my heart and I pray you do too! God is so more than money, more than a perfect day, etc. Oh my Jesus I want, I pray, I live to manifest the fullness of YOU. Thank you Jesus for your toward me.

Here is one more short detail story. I was asked to go to a wedding in Philadelphia. I called and made a reservation at a campground in Lancaster Pa. About thirty minutes later I decided to call Deb and James, some friends of mine. They have six children and live in a small motor home. I hadn't heard form them in months and just wanted to see how they were doing. Deb said they were in Boston and they are heading to Lancaster Pa next week. I jumped for joy and told her I will be there too. Thank you Jesus!

The following week we met. God is in the details. It turned out they got there a day ahead of me and on the day I was to arrive the people next to them left. The campsite next to them was available for any one and Deb said people drove by all day but for some reason no one took that site. I arrived in the early evening and was able to get the site right next to them. Thank you Jesus I love living in your details.

The next day we all went to tour a pretzel factory. The town it was in was built in the late eighteen hundreds so parking space for cars is a premium. I saw an open parking spot, one you didn't have to parallel park in. Deb pulled in and noticed the parking meter. No one had any change, so I said let me see if the meter has any time left on it. The meter had one hour and ten minutes left on it. The children and I were rejoicing, walking down the side walk signing and laughing saying, "That's my Jesus, that's my Jesus, thank you Jesus!" After the tour we walked back to the car and right as we got there, the timer on the meter went to zero time left. With God every detail is covered. Thank you Jesus! I love you too!

When I told this story to some friends they said Jesus always puts icing on your cake. I said you know I pray to walk with my Lord everyday and together we not only have icing on our cake but Jesus and I live in the icing! We swim in the icing! We eat the icing. Now that's a sweet detail and that's my Jesus!

Without Faith, It is Impossible to Please God

Lately in my quiet time with my Jesus, we have been talking about faith. Jesus loves faith. Jesus honors people of faith. For Jesus, faith is an action word and as you know Jesus told us, "Without faith it is impossible to please Him."

Hebrews 11:6 And without faith it is impossible to please him, for whoever would draw near to God must believe that he exists and that he rewards those who seek him.

Faith is very important to my Jesus. Faith is very important to us if we want to please Jesus. I believe faith is a lifestyle. I believe Jesus modeled a lifestyle of faith for us to model our life on. For me, faith is simply believing God loves you. Faith is trusting in God's love for us and faith in God is our hope for a better future. No walk with my Jesus would be complete without faith.

Jesus always praised people of faith. Jesus even gave us a list of people with great faith. Read Hebrews 11. I believe Hebrews 11 is open ended. I believe Jesus is still writing Hebrews 11 so use your faith to get into it. Listen to what Jesus said to His apostles when they ask for more faith.

Luke 17:5-6 And the apostles said unto the Lord, Increase our faith. And the Lord said, If ye had faith as a grain of mustard seed, ye might say unto this sycamine tree, Be thou plucked up by the root, and be thou planted in the sea; and it should obey you.

I am told the sycamine tree is the strongest tree of trees and the roots there of; are super strong. Jesus is telling us – *His apostles of today*, if we have faith as a grain of mustard seed Jesus will honor His words when we speak them.

Our faith will grow as we come to know Jesus Christ as our savior, leader, teacher and the protector of our eternal life. Seek to know Jesus personally and you will preach the kingdom is at hand because you will know it is.

As I talk to Jesus more about faith, it seems clear there are two categories of faith. First is what I call fun faith. *Fun faith* is casting out devils, healing the sick, raising people from the dead. These actions of faith are what I think of as fun faith. I call it fun faith because it is literally fun to do and it is fun to see the miracles. Jesus talked about the joy the apostles had when they were sent out to do miracles. Watching Jesus perform on His Word is definitely fun and you too will do miracles by faith in Jesus when you call on His name.

The second category of faith is what I call *true faith* or the *true belief* category. For now let us look at what Jesus told the apostles about faith.

Luke 10:17 And the seventy returned again with joy, saying, Lord, even the devils are subject unto us through thy name.

We see here the apostles were filled with Joy when they saw the power in proclaiming the name of Jesus. We too will be excited and filled with joy when we call on the name of Jesus and see miracles happen *fun faith*. The apostles were commanded or commissioned by Jesus to go into every city and preach the Word and heal the sick therein. Guess what? We have the same commission.

The problem with fun faith is our faith can sometimes be defined by seeing the miracles. Fun faith can sometimes be shallow faith. That is if we don't see what we commanded to happen, say a miracle healing, we sometimes lose our faith and stop commanding things to happen. Our faith is determined by our circumstances or by the results we see and not by actual true faith. Therefore, I believe fun faith is different than true faith because true faith is not determined by what we see. True faith is determined by what we believe and not what we see.

45

Please don't let your past dictate your future. Read these Scriptures and you will see the faith of the apostles at this point in their walk was in seeing miracles. I know this because when the apostles could not cast the demon out of a boy, their faith faded like the wind. Jesus said to them

Matthew 17:14-17 And when they were come to the multitude, there came to him a certain man, kneeling down to him, and saying, Lord, have mercy on my son: for he is lunatick, and sore vexed: for oftimes he falleth into the fire, and oft into the water. And I brought him to thy disciples, and they could not cure him. Then Jesus answered and said, O faithless and perverse generation, how long shall I be with you? how long shall I suffer you? bring him hither to me.

In my heart I hear these words *O faithless and perverse generation, how long shall I be with you? How long shall I suffer you? Bring him hither to me.* And think how upset Jesus must have been to even say them. For me, these words prove Jesus was a man and He was human. My heart cries upon hearing these words. The torment in the heart of Jesus came out in His words. I believe there had to still be a look of love on the face of Jesus toward the apostles because the apostles did not get upset and walk away. They could have said, "He called us faithless and perverse generation after we walked with Him three years. The heck with this. I'm out of here." I believe and thank God they accepted the words of Jesus because they knew the love of Jesus.

Think about this: We humans read faces really well. We can tell at a glance if someone is mad, angry, sad, depressed or in pain. It is harder for us to read the face of love and caring because there are people who are deceitful in their heart and their looks. I believe Jesus carried such a true look of love, peace and hope, that one glance made you want what Jesus had. These are the looks that make us a peculiar chosen people – a generation set apart to do the work of His kingdom. We believers will carry an awareness of the love of Jesus and in doing so we will be made aware of the peace or lack of peace as we enter someone's home.

Luke 10:5-6 And into whatsoever house ye enter, first say, Peace be to this house. And if the son of peace be there, your peace shall rest upon it: if not, it shall turn to you again.

1 Peter 2:9 But ye are a chosen generation, a royal priesthood, an holy nation, a peculiar people; that ye should shew forth the praises of him who hath called you out of darkness into his marvellous light

I love being peculiar or being set apart. I have joined a royal priesthood and I willingly lay down the dung of this world and I pray to be eternally peculiar, chosen and loved by my Lord. Jesus lived and modeled this life for us. So if some words come out of your heart that sound human, remember we are loved and forgiven the moment we ask forgiveness. Jesus knew His Father still loved Him and our Father picked Jesus right up and Jesus continued

Matthew 17:18-20 And Jesus rebuked the devil; and he departed out of him: and the child was cured from that very hour. Then came the disciples to Jesus apart, and said, Why could not we cast him out? And Jesus said unto them, Because of your unbelief: for verily I say unto you, If ye have faith as a grain of mustard seed, ye shall say unto this mountain, Remove hence to yonder place; and it shall remove; and nothing shall be impossible unto you.

Remember the apostles had not been filled with the Holy Spirit yet, so they didn't have a direct line to Jesus like we do. If the apostles wanted to talk to Jesus they had to go find Jesus. If the apostles wanted to talk to Jesus alone they had to wait until Jesus was alone to talk to Him. Contrast their relationship with ours. We are filled with the Holy Spirit if we believe. We have 24/7 relationship if we believe. Jesus comes with all the gifts of the Holy Spirit operating 24/7 through us if we believe. We have a commission to call on the name of Jesus in faith, and Jesus honors His Word. Please just believe like a child.

Come on people, Jesus gave us His all – *nothing shall be impossible unto you.* These are the words of Jesus to us. I believe them by faith for Jesus said them. I focus on my Jesus and I simply cannot doubt. If you have any doubts simply do what the apostles did – go right to Jesus and ask Him for help. Jesus simply prayed for His apostles to receive His love and Jesus continues praying for us also.

Look at what else Jesus said to the apostles when they came back all excited.

Luke 10:17-18 And the seventy returned again with joy, saying, Lord, even the devils are subject unto us through thy name. And he said unto them, I beheld Satan as lightning fall from heaven.

Why on Earth did Jesus say that to the apostles? I mean, they had just gotten back from their missionary trip and were all excited about devils being subject to them in the name of Jesus. I believe Jesus was telling the apostles that what they saw really is not that big deal because Jesus beheld Satan fall as lighting, like a flash of light here one minute and gone the next, to Jesus this was not a big deal. Then Jesus said:

Luke 10:19 Behold, I give unto you power to tread on serpents and scorpions, and over all the power of the enemy: and nothing shall by any means hurt you.

Here I believe Jesus is telling the apostles that they believed because they saw the results of calling on the name of Jesus. Then Jesus went on to tell the apostles you simply must believe I give you the authority to trample on snakes and scorpions and to destroy the enemy's power no matter what you see in the flesh or your faith will be shallow. In Luke 10:19, I believe Jesus was reinforcing the fact that Jesus is the author and finisher of our faith. Jesus is the power we are to believe in but we are not to be swayed by the circumstances we see or our faith will be shallow.

I believe Jesus has a higher level of faith for those of us that truly believe in His love for us. I have casts out devils before, but I have never even thought of actually destroying the power of the devil until this very moment – *and over all the power of the enemy*. This book is written for me as much as everyone else. I am growing up in the Word of God and the power we have with faith in His name and I pray you are too.

I believe we must have faith enough to believe in the words of Jesus. When we believe in His words, "Nothing by any means can hurt you," the evil spirit of fear will leave and the spirit of boldness will come into our life. I hope you see we have what we believe. Faith comes from walking in the revelation of Gods love for us, not our love for Him but His love for us. Then Jesus tells His apostles what a big deal really is in Luke 10:20.

Luke 10:20 Notwithstanding in this rejoice not, that the spirits are subject unto you; but rather rejoice, because your names are written in heaven.

I believe Jesus knew we humans have a tendency to become puffed up with power or possibly Jesus thought we might think we are the ones doing the casting out. I believe Jesus told the apostles not to be excited or rejoicing about the evil spirits being subject to you because Jesus had a far more important reason for coming to earth. In a word, the reason Jesus came was for us to communicate with Him 24/7. Jesus knew through communicating with Him we will become His loving ambassadors here on earth. Jesus answered every question the apostles had and He will answer your question too.

I believe if for some heavenly reason when we call on the name of Jesus and we don't see healing or if the devil doesn't come out or the person doesn't come back to life, our faith in God's Word plummets and we will stop using the power and authority Jesus gave us in His name. We are so blessed because even with some doubt we have the gift of the Holy Spirit in us and Jesus knew we needed an open line of communication so He gave us one.

Jesus gave us the ability to communicate with Him so He could keep His love alive in us. Remember Jesus didn't give up on the apostles and Jesus will not give up on us either and remember Jesus forgave the apostles for their doubt of belief and we are forgiven also. I hope you see forgiveness is an example of true love. Yes, Jesus loved us first and Jesus prayed for us to simply believe Him.

For a heavenly walk with Jesus we need to realize in Luke 10:20 Jesus is telling us our faith needs to be rooted in the love Jesus has for us. Jesus is telling us we need to know our name is written in heaven. For the knowledge of knowing our name is written in Heaven is far more important then judging our faith by our circumstances. When we believe we are loved by God and when we believe our names are written in heaven, then and only then will all things be possible for us. The really big deal Jesus is impressing on us is we are loved by God and we will realize it when we know in our heart that our names are written in heaven.

Jesus knew His people need security. Believers who know they are loved and know their names are written in heaven have security and rewards. Read John and see for yourself.

John 10:27 My sheep hear my voice, and I know them, and they follow me:

Please notice we hear His voice, and he knows us and we follow Him. That is not just singing to Him or praying a list of earthly dung we need. Following is laying down our time to do the work of His kingdom. I am not sure where worship became singing or prayer became a list of needs but I pray for discernment about these things.

John 10:28-30 And I give unto them eternal life; and they shall never perish, neither shall any man pluck them out of my hand. My Father, which gave them me, is greater than all; and no man is able to pluck them out of my Father's hand. I and my Father are one.

We hear His voice. We know Jesus loves us and we follow Him. Jesus gives us eternal life. We know we will never perish. No man can pluck us out of His hand. Sounds like a great retirement plan and some really great security to me. Yes! Count me in! The two requirements are to believe in God – that is to walk by faith and not by sight and Jesus said for us to follow Him.

Please think about the relationship Jesus had with His Father. Jesus knew His Father loved Him. Jesus knew His name was written in Heaven. Jesus knew no man could pluck Him out of His

Father's hand and Jesus knew the trial set before Him and yet Jesus never doubted His Father's love for Him. The faith of Jesus in His Father's love pleased His Father and gave His Father great joy. Let us look how our walk can please Jesus and our Father and give them great joy.

Luke 10:21 In that hour the Holy Spirit filled Jesus with joy. Jesus said, "I praise you, Father, Lord of heaven and earth, for hiding these things from wise and intelligent people and revealing them to little children. Yes, Father, this is what pleased you."

Here we see how easy it is to fill Jesus with joy. Upon hearing, the apostles believed and seeing them walk in the power and authority He gave them Jesus was filled with Joy. Yes, when we use the power and authority Jesus gave us in faith we will not only see healings, devils cast out and people brought back from the dead but we will literally bring joy to Jesus and through Jesus to our Father. That makes me want to do some joy jumping.

The joy we bring to our Lord by *believing in His word* goes way beyond singing and listing to pleasing sermons on Sunday morning. I really cannot understand how doing something that takes absolutely no faith, like singing on Sunday mornings is supposed to bring joy to God. The joy we bring to Jesus by believing in the power we have in His name is what I call true worshipping and we read in Luke 10:21 true faith fills Jesus and our Father God with joy. Yes our simple belief that Jesus and Father God love us will make all things possible and we truly bring joy to God.

Jesus asks us to follow Jesus like the apostles did. That is we walk in His power through faith in Him. I live in a camper, I travel around the United States and I am in a lot of churches of all denominations. It seems every Sunday Service I go to has at least three worship songs. Some worship services I have been to has the entire service singing to God about how much we love Him. I leave these services thinking they have nothing in them but empty songs. There is no testifying of God's Word. There is no call for anyone to do anything except come back next week and sing some more and hope the Holy Spirit gives us a feeling of a good feeling.

51

It seems to me these *singing worship services* are empty of substance because there is no call for anyone to come to know God more intimately. If you are in the hospital dying of cancer right now and I came into your hospital room and started singing 'You are worthy Lord, I love you Lord, you are wonderful Lord, you are a good Lord, I love you Lord,' would you even know God is a healer? Would you get up and be healed?

At Sunday service we should be edifying each other. Helping each other build our faith with testifying. I hear preachers say "Don't worry, I read the book and in the end it says we win," and everyone in the congregation cheers. But I ask you, how do we win? I don't think Jesus won by singing to His Father.

Revelation 12:10-11 And I heard a loud voice saying in heaven, Now is come salvation, and strength, and the kingdom of our God, and the power of his Christ: for the accuser of our brethren is cast down, which accused them before our God day and night. And they overcame him by the blood of the Lamb, and by the word of their testimony; and they loved not their lives unto the death.

Read this Scripture again and again. We overcome the devil by our faith in the blood of Jesus and our faith in God gives us boldness and boldness gives us testimonies. I believe God is describing how to worship. I believe God is a God of action. Faith is an action word, not just a song. Our churches should be filled with testimonies. My God is just as powerful today as ever and my God wants us to prove His power by our faith in Him.

Instead of testimonies in churches we have what I call faithless songs, 'I love you Jesus, I love you Jesus, and I love you Jesus. Okay, I feel great, where should we go eat, but hurry the football game starts in an hour.' I have been in churches where the preachers cut the service short so everyone can get home to watch the stupid game. If the game is so important then start the service early that Sunday. But please I am begging you don't cut short the hour or two we give to the Lord.

If my house was falling down around me, and I had equipped my children with everything they need to fix the problem and they were too lazy or too busy to do the simple things I ask of them.

Well, my children could sing to me 24/7 about how much they love me and all there singing would be totally worthless to me. Jesus could have spent His whole life singing love songs to His Father and we would still be under the law, killing and burning animals as a blood sacrifice and Jesus would have flunked His test.

Please follow Jesus by walking the walk Jesus modeled for us. Worship Jesus by believing in Him and being His love to everyone you meet. Worship Jesus by asking Jesus what He needs to be done today and then making His priority your top priority. Dung is dung and it stinks but the love of Jesus is true love and it transforms hearts, cities, towns, and countries. We don't need Jesus to fill the atmosphere. We need to believe Him when He said we are His atmosphere. Please understand that He is in you so He is already here.

In Luke 10:21, Jesus reveals to us how He sees us. Jesus refers to us as *little children*. We believers do not need to be the 'wise and intelligent' people of this earth. I believe Jesus said this because the wise and intelligent people almost always want to know how things work and why things work and be able to explain how things work, Jesus said knowledge like that puffs us up.

Consider this: if you need to know how things work, and why things work and if you can explain how things work; you really need no faith in God for those things and you don't need God. The very first temptation of Eve was to become as god. Read what the devil said to Eve.

Genesis 3:5 For God doth know that in the day ye eat thereof, then your eyes shall be opened, and ye shall be as gods, knowing good and evil.

The devil is still tempting us to be as gods to ourselves. When we need to explain things like creation we are trying to be a god to ourselves. I wonder why there is even a need to know or explain things like the evolution stuff. I mean, when you share your knowledge of evolution does it help others live a better life? Will evolution knowledge improve the world or will that knowledge stop wars?

One thing evolutionist and followers of Jesus Christ have in common is we both need faith to believe the way we do. Evolutionists need faith in man's findings to believe in evolution and we followers of Jesus need faith in God to believe in His teachings. In all beliefs you need faith in something but faith in Father God and His Son Jesus will make the world a better place to live.

If evolutionists persuade us to believe in their evolution junk then we don't need God because we know how we came to be. We are god to ourselves. The devil has not changed his question in thousands of years.

Faith and Belief

No one can explain healings except to say they are miraculous or supernatural and those words just describe healings they don't explain them. Try to explain how or why we command devils to come out of someone and the devil has to flee. Try to explain how or why we command the dead to come back to life and death flees. We followers of Jesus simply speak these things to happen and Jesus makes them happen. These things all require faith in God so our belief in God is the manifested miracles by our faith in God. I believe we can be wise and intelligent in our belief of Jesus and with simple child like faith in Jesus we make Jesus and Father God very joyful. Now that's my Jesus!

Another difference or distinction between the wise and intelligent people and us His little children believers is the work of Jesus only requires faith. I have no idea how Jesus can be in Heaven and in my heart at the same time but I believe by faith that He is. I have no idea how to explain a miracle to someone but by faith I believe it happens. I have no idea how the same spirit of Jesus can be in all those who believe at the same time but by faith I believe that He is. I have no idea how God created the world in six days but by faith I believe He did. Jesus said to come to Him as child. I believe the way I do and to some people I look childish in my beliefs but to my Jesus I am His child who believes.

My simple belief in Jesus and Father God make me seem childish to others but my simple beliefs make me available to fellowship with God and be His ambassador to all I meet. In Genesis God said He created us for fellowship, so I think it is very important to make time to fellowship with Him. You see, I believe in God so I don't have to figure out every detail of my life. I hear His voice because I believe God wants to talk to me. My beliefs are probably childish and stupid to the wise and intelligent of this world but my whole hearted wise and intelligent faith I bring joy to my Father and my Jesus and I heal the sick, raise the dead and cast out devils.

In Luke 10:21, Jesus even praises His Father for revealing these things to babies or little children. I believe Jesus uses the term little children to describe us believers because when we believers come as little children we come with an open heart. We come not needing an explanation of how God works or how God created the world in six days because we childish believers simply believe. A child will come with full expectancy that God will work, that God did work and God is working through us believers today, tomorrow and forever. A child is teachable, a child will look you right in the eye and a child will receive and believe the words of love from our Father God and Jesus. If a child knows he is loved a child will listen to and follow His Father without any doubt.

As a childish believer I pray without an answer – that is I pray knowing God is the answer and I pray knowing God will answer my prayers. I never pray in doubt like 'If it be your will Father, please heal this person.' I read His Holy Bible so I know the will of the Father. So if I pray and if nothing seems to happen I already know in my heart it will happen and I will stand in faith forever that it will happen. This might sound childish but I believe my faith makes my Jesus and my Father really joyful.

I am a child of God and I love being a child of God. I cannot explain how the things that go on around believers happen but I know they are of God. I know the most important life lesson we will ever learn is how to please God and how to bring Joy into His life. So if you are trying to figure God out, please stop trying to figure God out and simply enjoy Him loving you because you are His child and you are His creation, you are made in His image and likeness. I beg you to listen for his voice, to let the Holy Spirit of God transform you into who He created you to be. Yes, please let God love you.

Here is a story of a man I met in a campground who had creation all figured out. The man I met not too long ago was a professor in a college. He taught evolution and the Big Bang stuff. When he saw my bumper sticker *Coffee Time With Jesus* and realized I was a believer in Jesus he came over to talk to me. He made it his mission that night to convince me that evolution is real. He talked to me for over two hours, explaining his point of view and told me about the scientist he knew from around the world and how all these scientist came to the same conclusions, the world evolved over thousands and thousands of years.

When he had exhausted himself I looked him right in the eye and said thank you for explaining your beliefs to me but my Jesus said in His book God created the world in six days and I believe Jesus and so I moved on from all this science stuff a long time ago. By moving on I have learned how my Jesus loves me and wants to flow through me to heal the sick and raise the dead and cast out devils. You know, none of these things are possible to those who believe the way you do. So if you want me to prove to you my belief is real I will by simply calling on the name of Jesus and then by watching Jesus prove beyond any scientific reasoning He is real.

You see I will not argue with anyone whether Jesus is real or not. I simply let my Jesus flow through me and He proves beyond any doubt He is real. I can prove Jesus is real in seconds, not hours and I don't need hundreds of scientist to back me up. I have one back up and His name is Jesus. Jesus wrote one book the Holy Bible and it has stood the test of time. I believe Jesus and I will not be swayed by man's knowledge even if man's knowledge proves me right. You see, I don't need man's knowledge to prove me right because I already believe in my Jesus and I know my Jesus is real and He is right. My beliefs are so simple to me because I believe.

I know this is childish thinking to a man with your knowledge but to me it is a simple way of life. I have no doubts, no fears, and I know all things are possible for me because I believe in the truth of Jesus. Does all your knowledge give you peace? Does sharing your knowledge bring joy into your life? Does your knowledge bring hope for a better future to anyone? If a murderer was pointing a gun at you right now would all your studying and all your research protect you? Does all your knowledge comforts you or gives you love?

My Jesus protects me. I am comforted by knowing my Jesus loves me and the love of Jesus gives me hope, peace joy, and strength. The best part of knowing Jesus is knowing Jesus loves me and I am childishly in love with Him and His love for me will overflow to everyone I meet. I childishly believe Jesus and for my belief in Jesus I have peace, I have hope, I have joy, and I know I am loved by my Father so I Have no needs.

Knowledge is good and being wise is good when used to build the Kingdom of God. When knowledge and intelligence are only used to make yourself right and someone else wrong. I believe they become bad or displeasing to God. The big difference between my belief and yours is my Jesus will prove He is real and your belief is only backed up with data that is based on some mans scientific findings.

I guess I can sum up this whole conversation up by saying we all have faith in something. But my faith has direction, my faith in is alive and real and is life transforming and my faith has a reward and a promise of eternal life. Please think about where your faith in evolution will take you? The best answer I have gotten to the question 'Where does your knowledge in evolution take you?' is an evolutionist I met, once said he wanted to be buried under a tree so he could become tree food. Now there in is a great reward for all your learning and there is a hope for a greener future. Come on everybody think green and make sure you use the right laundry detergent.

I wonder who told the evolutionist the tree needed food in the first place. Maybe we should dig up all the body's in all cemeteries and turn them into a great untapped green food and then we could save the planet. Please choose well for the difference is heaven or worse than just a hope of becoming tree food it could be hell. I said could be hell because I don't judge but I know the judge personally and the judge loves me.

Jesus never argued and neither will I.

The Goal is to Walk with Jesus

The goal of the Christian Churches should line up with the goal of Father God and Jesus. What was the goal Jesus had in mind when He came to earth? In my Holy Bible, there is a story about when John the Baptist sent two of his disciples to ask Jesus 'Are you the one we are to follow or do we look for another?' Jesus didn't preach to them. Jesus didn't say 'John the Baptist and I need to have some meetings to find common ground where we can build a church.' He simply said to them 'Come follow me around today and see for yourself.' At the end of the hour, Jesus said 'Now go and report to John what you have seen and heard, the lame walk, the blind see, devils have been cast out, the dead rise up and He preached the kingdom of God is at hand boldly.' May I add this was just an average hour in the life of my Jesus. Do you think the goal of Jesus was to build thousands of denominations with sub denominations?

Luke 7:20-23 When the men were come unto him, they said, John Baptist hath sent us unto thee, saying, Art thou he that should come? or look we for another? And in that same hour he cured many of their infirmities and plagues, and of evil spirits; and unto many that were blind he gave sight. Then Jesus answering said unto them, Go your way, and tell John what things ye have seen and heard; how that the blind see, the lame walk, the lepers are cleansed, the deaf hear, the dead are raised, to the poor the gospel is preached. And blessed is he, whosoever shall not be offended in me.

Hmm… Isn't that crazy? Jesus didn't try to persuade John's followers with lofty words or arguments, scientific findings, man's knowledge, test results… Although I am sure He could. Jesus just went about His kingdom work and let John's men observe. Here again Jesus gave us a really good example to follow. I will follow Jesus. Will you?

I believe this was just another hour in the life of my Jesus. To live as Jesus lived is our goal. We are to walk as Jesus walked – healing, comforting, bring sight, casting out devils, raising the dead and all this is possible with simple belief that Jesus Christ and Father God love us. For us, to believe we must know and be established in our heart that the love of Father God and Jesus are real. We must know we can have the Holy Spirit of Father God and Jesus in us. Jesus said in His Word I only do what I see my Father do.

John 5:19-20 So Jesus said to them, "Truly, truly, I say to you, the Son can do nothing of his own accord, but only what he sees the Father doing. For whatever the Father does, that the Son does likewise. For the Father loves the Son and shows him all that he himself is doing. And greater works than these will he show him, so that you may marvel."

This is how we walk with my Jesus. This is the Good News to proclaim to the world. We can become Sons of God just as Jesus the man became a Son of God when He was baptized. We too can be baptized and ask our Father to adopt us into the kingdom of walking as a son of God and walking with the Spirit of Father God in us. Jesus was a talking; walking, miracle everyday and proved to anyone who would believe in Him they could talk and walk the same way He did. Ask our Father to adopt you and you to will receive the baptism of life into the life of Jesus and knowing Him intimately. Yes we are Sons of God who are loved by God and as sons of God we will do everything we see our Brother do. All we need to do is believe!

In John 5:20 Jesus tells us why He did what the Father showed Him:

John 5:20 For the Father loves the Son and shows him all that he himself is doing. And greater works than these will he show him, so that you may marvel.

Yes, the Father loves the Son. Guess what we born again believers are? Yes you are so right. We are Sons of God the Father and the receivers of His love. We can do what Jesus did because living in the Love of the Father like Jesus did is the goal our Jesus came to show and share with us. So what else must we beloved Sons of God do? I believe walking in the love of Jesus is the entire picture Jesus came to give us. I know that is just too simple of a message for most of us, so let us look at some details as to how and what this walk we are on looks like to Jesus.

I read in the Word that Jesus said He came to set the captives free. Jesus said it and I believe Jesus! Setting the captives free is part of the goal. I guess we could ask "How did the coming of Jesus set the captives free? Did not Father God already do that? He led the Israelites out of captivity and did not Father God already show us His great strength, His thunderous voice, and His might. Did not Father God already show us miracles so great, we are still in awe? Are miracles what set us free?" I believe miracles are just enticements to come to know God. Miracles have been performed by God to show us how much He loves us but miracles do not set us free. True freedom comes from relationship with God and knowing God loves us.

Shortly after setting the Israelites free, God ask Moses to prepare the people to come up on the mountain. God wanted His people to meet Him. I believe Father God wanted to fellowship with us His creation and that is why He invited us to come up on the mountain so our Father God could talk to us all. It is true God uses miracles to prove His love for us is real and to show us He wants a loving relationship with us but the goal is not just more miracles. The goal is the transformations of nonbelievers into believers.

I remember talking to Jesus and Father God about Moses being on the mountain for three days. I ask Jesus what it was like in heaven when He and Father saw their chosen people worshipping a golden image shortly after God had performed all the miracles to set them free. I mean God send plagues, frogs, locus, parted the red sea and drown the soldiers chasing the Israelites. I wondered what else God could do to get His people to believe He loved them.

Then in my mind I pictured Father God and Jesus sitting on their thrones with disappointment on their faces as they saw the Israelites making a gold image to worship. Then Jesus looked at His Father and said, "Send me Father, I will personalize your love to them. I will heal one person at a time, I will cast demons out one person at a time, and I will raise them from the dead one person at a time. I will personalize your love to them and maybe then they will believe how personable your love is to each one individually."

I believe the goal of Father God in sending His Son was to show how personally He loves us. Father showed His love for us by letting His Son be a living model of His love and by allowing His son to be crucified for our sins. This made Jesus the ultimate example of laying down His life for another, the ultimate sacrifice for sin and the ultimate lover of mankind. Jesus came and opened personal communication. Him and Father gave us their Holy Spirit and showed us how we too are to fulfill the law and so much more. I believe Jesus achieved the goals by knowing without doubting His Father's love for Him.

Here we are 2000 plus years later arguing over denominations and who is right instead of simply being the model of our Father's love Jesus came and modeled to us. Here we are watching television, spending time on the internet and by spending so much time on these things we are making these things our modern golden idols like those of years past. When I read about the golden idols of old, I thought how stupid can one be. I mean they were worshiping something they made for themselves. But now I live in campgrounds and see people spend hours getting their satellite thing working and then they leave two days later. Yes they will spend hours setting up their dish so they can watch television. I think do we really need a $500,000 motor home to watch television?

We have been blessed, rewarded, showered on and we can walk with the Lord in us and flowing trough us and we have the Holy Spirit to teach us and talk to us and transform us; we are loved 24/7. People everything else is dung. The way I see our world, Jesus really isn't asking us to give up much. I guess to some people dung is a lot to give up especially if you are still paying for it.

Some people I talk too think the goal will be achieved by more church planting or starting another denomination with what they believe has more of God's truth. For me, the goal is simply for us who believe to become the love of Jesus! We simply must become aware Jesus came and laid down His life to show us how much He and Father God love us. We simply need to know Father God loves us and to know we can build their kingdom by letting their love flow through us. Become a willing vessel of the love of Father God by becoming like Jesus and you become the goal.

Jesus did not come to start a denomination. We are not to be a denomination of Jesus Christ. I simply will not be defined and limited by some mans interpolation of a denomination. We believers are a people set apart by Jesus when we walk in the love of Jesus. We believers simply must walk out the life Jesus modeled for us. I believe my Brother Jesus Christ came to earth so we would see the life He lived, a life of no worry, no fear, and full of hope, faith and love. Would you like to be worry-free? Jesus even paid His taxes with money from a fish mouth. Now that is living worry free.

Yes, Jesus wanted us to see the love our Father God has so we too could become the love of God the Father and be worry-free. Thank you Jesus and I will prove my love for Jesus by my belief that Jesus can make me and actually wants to transform me into His loving forgiveness to all. Now that is worry-free.

Miracles are an important part of God's ministry. God uses miracles to show us His power and might. I believe He shows us how He can protect us by miracles. I believe God removes fear with miracles and He removes sickness, pain, death, and devils with miracles. God repairs our broken heart with miracles. With that in mind, you could say miracles could set us free. I believe there is a bigger picture here. I believe the bigger picture is the motive of God's miracles. I believe miracles help us focus on Jesus. They give us a desire to know Him more and with these desires we will want to hear His voice and our focus will allow us to discern his voice. Each one of these desires will bring us into a closer walk with our Lord.

You might be thinking 'I am in need of a miracle right now. I have stood in faith for years. I have been praying for by some of the big men of faith and Jesus has never showed His love for me with a miracle. I am in pain right now and every day. So why will not Father God heal me?' Have you asked these questions? Are these questions spoken in your church?

Personally, I refuse to speak for my Father God. I will not try to explain anything that I don't understand. I will tell you for sure God is capable. God desires for you to know He loves you and I believe Jesus went through all He did to prove His love for us and for are greater good.

Please believe you can have a personal relationship with Jesus and go for it! Please don't let your circumstances hold you back. God honors His Word so quote His Word for Jesus to hear. Jesus said His word will not come back void. Remember complaining is not praying. Focus on Jesus and tell the problem about God's word, you don't need to tell God about your problem. Believe God and everything around you will change.

I prayed and stood in faith for eleven years. I carried my Jenny everywhere we went and took care of her seven days a week for almost eleven years. Jenny couldn't talk, walk, feed herself, change herself, bath herself or dress herself. I had the big names in healing ministries pray for her and her condition continued to worsen but somehow through all of those 4015 days I saw the love of Jesus in our walk every day.

During this time I was bitten by a brown recluse spider three times. I had eruptions from it. For over four years and never went to a doctor. I knew my Jesus was taking care of me and He did. I knew my Jesus was taking care of my Jenny and He did.

I guess you could say the love of Jesus didn't manifest in my Jenny as the miracle I prayed for. But His love did see me through and gave me the inner strength to carry my Jenny and to care for my Jenny. His love for us gave Jenny the strength to love me in ways that are beyond my understanding. After eleven years of daily caring for my Jenny, on April 27th 2013 I was blessed to have my Jenny in our camper sitting on my lap and while holding her in my arms, I literally watched her smile at me and saw her tears of joy as her spirit went to her final reward. Although my dream was for Jenny to be healed here on Earth and be with me, I was able with the help of my Jesus to praise God for His decision.

All I can tell is with faith in God we will receive the grace we need to see us through this life. Our faith in knowing God loves us is actually a greater display of His love then the miracle we think we want. No matter what the circumstances of our life look like here on Earth, I believe with all my heart my Jesus sees the picture completely from start to finish. So I keep my faith in Him and even though I sometimes miss my Jenny so much I think my heart will break. I simply hold fast to my belief that the love of Jesus will see me through. I know in my heart Jesus Himself is here with me so I don't doubt and will not ever doubt His love for me. My personal goal in life is to never doubt the love of Father God and Jesus have for me.

Miracles are a great tool God uses to bring us to know Him. Miracles are not the end all to His expression of love for us. I believe grace is a bigger miracle then anything physical we can ever experience. If your prayers start with the word *why*, I think you might want to rethink your prayer life.

I really don't think asking God *why* is a prayer of faith. It is simply a question of a nonbeliever. I believe prayers should start with 'Thank you Jesus for being for me and with me. I know without a doubt you have an answer for my prayer and so I refuse to spend my time trying to figure out your answer. But instead, I just thank you Jesus you are the answer and I thank you Jesus for bring heaven to Earth for me.'

Like I said earlier in this writing, I don't even have a desire to understand or explain everything God does or doesn't do. Understanding like that would just be way too much information for me right now. I just know by faith that God will explain things to me when I need to know it and I will wait patiently until I see Him if I have questions when I get there. I know without a doubt that God answers our prayers and when it comes to answering prayer; the word *maybe* is not a word in His vocabulary.

I would like to take a moment to answer the most asked question I had while I cared for my Jenny. Anyone that knew me before Jenny got sick witness the changes in me as I became Jenny's caregiver. The question always came up, "Do you think Jesus used Jenny's sickness to grow you up in the Lord?" My answer is simply NO!

I see Jesus as a big God – a God with unlimited love, a God with unlimited resources, a God who will move a mountain and slay the giants in our path. When you see God this way, you simply know God has no need what so ever to put a sickness on anyone to help someone else get to know Him better. God loves me so much. God simply took a man that was too busy to talk to Him and gave me time to come to know Him. God revealed to me His love for me was my strength, my hope and I could put all my trust in Him and with this revelation I came to walk in faith. I know God loves me!

I praise God Jenny and I was able to spend the last eleven years of her life together 24/7. I see this as a huge blessing. For more information on our walk together please read *Love Never Fails*.

Why Did Jesus Come?

Some time ago I ask Jesus this question. It seems everywhere I go people tell their version as to why Jesus came. I decided to go right to my Jesus and I knew He would tell me first hand why He came. Jesus led me into John.

John 17:21 That they all may be one; as thou, Father, art in me, and I in thee, that they also may be one in us: that the world may believe that thou hast sent me.

I believe we have the answer to the question 'Why did Jesus come?' in one word – BELIEVE. For us to gain eternal life we must believe in a God who has eternal life. I also believe God created us for fellowship with Him. Jesus proved by coming we are very important to Him and to our Father. Jesus came to give us the Holy Spirit. Yes, we have the very SAME Spirit of Father God and Jesus in us so we may be one with them as they are one in each other. This is so very important: we simply must believe we can have the Holy Spirit of Father God and Jesus in us. I believe. Do you?

To walk as Jesus walked seemed impossible to me at first. Then after reading in the Holy Bible how we have the same Holy Spirit as Father God and Jesus in us now born again believers. I began to realize they love us so much they gave us everything we need to walk as Jesus did by giving us their same Holy Spirit. I have no idea how that happens but I believe! I know for some people this takes a lot of faith to believe but please simply believe by faith for this is the Word of God.

With this revelation of how much God wants to spend time with me and knowing Father God and Jesus live in me, my life started to change. Their love came into me with their Holy Spirit and they are so gentle to me, the change was painless. People started to see the changes in me. I loved who Jesus was transforming me into. Then I realized "Hey, I'm supposed to love myself. Jesus told us in His word to love thy neighbor as yourself. I have the Holy Spirit of the love of God living in me. How can I let my past bother me now that truth has come? Jesus loves me and I am special to my Jesus."

Yes I have the Holy Spirit of truth living in me. Please believe the words of Jesus in John 17:21 for they are true. Take them into your heart; claim them as your own and live as Jesus lived. If you want to know Jesus as personal and as intimate as possible and if you want to know the truth let sets us free please ask Jesus and Father God into your heart and you will see a painless change take place in your heart.

You will look in the mirror in the morning and see a beautiful reflection of someone who loves you looking back at you. I believe; do you? I call Jesus my Jesus but don't worry; we are into sharing.

When I ask Father God and Jesus into my heart, they came with a peace I didn't understand at first. The peace they came with took fear away. I wanted to share this new love in me but I didn't know how. They showed me the knowledge of knowing they love me is more important for me to know than any other knowledge you can gain. You want peace in your life? Try believing God really loves you. True Peace is truly knowing God dwells in you.

I don't know everything but I know the one who does. That is peace.

I want my children and loved ones in heaven and I don't know how to make that happen but I know the one who does. That is peace. I have heard of some major changes coming for America and the world and that should be scary but I have peace about it because I know the Prince of Peace and they live in me. That is peace. Yes fear has been replaced with the love of my Father God and my Jesus living in me.

All this peace is totally beyond my understanding and I am at peace about that also because Paul said to the Philippians:

Philippians 4:7   and the peace of God, which surpasses all understanding, will guard your hearts and minds through Christ Jesus.

Then in Mark 9:23 Jesus says:

Mark 9:23   Jesus said to him, "If you can believe, all things are possible to him who believes."

If you make the conscience decision to let the Holy Spirit of God into your heart you will walk a new walk and live in heavenly peace here on earth. You might be asking yourself why Jesus came. And the answer is that so the world may believe! We have been given a choice and we are choosing life and death by the priorities we choose. I choose to seek my Heavenly Father and my brother Jesus with my whole heart and my whole heart and my whole heart became full of His love. I chose well. Thanks to my Jesus living in me.

Freedom to Choose

Having the Holy Spirit in your heart does not change your freedom to choose. I have asked God into my heart and I know for sure they are in my heart. But every day I live comes with thousands of little decisions to make. I can choose everyday to glorify God by the decisions I make or I can choose to make life about me and bring glory to myself.

We can be filled with the Holy Spirit and still not listening to the Holy Spirit. This is the choice we can make every day to listen or not to listen to the Holy Spirit of God. When I was younger, I was in debt, I had a mortgage payment on our house most of my life, I drove old cars and didn't use credit cards, so I only had one debt. I felt good about not being in as much debt as everyone else I knew. I justified my debt in my mind but somewhere down deep inside I hated the fact I was in debt.

I even prayed for the Lord to help me make the payments on my debt. I would get a check in my spirit every time I prayed about my debt. I cannot speak for others but my debt drove me crazy. I even blamed God for my debt. I told God if I had a better job or if people would just pay me what I am worth or if you Lord would get me out of debt I would have more time to be with you Lord. Yes when I was young I often prayed the problem.

That really is not much of a prayer is it? My motives were not really honorable. But guess what? God gave me some choices and with the help of my Jesus and with His love in my heart, I started listening to the Holy Spirit. I chose a debt-free way of life. Now I am free of debt and I serve one master and I have never been more joyful in my life. We have choices to make every day but now that I know the Lord wants to spend time with me, the choices have become so much easier.

Now I am debt-free and I have time to have Coffee With My Jesus. Jesus told me he wanted me to have Coffee Time With Jesus every day. Now I make time for my precious Coffee Time With Jesus and I would not trade that time for all the money in the world.

I believe the biggest blessing anyone can receive from God in this world is a steadfast desire to become one with God. I say this because all the circumstances and all the junk of this world that I thought I needed really only took me away from a desire to know God. Now I walk in this new freedom of being junk-less and I spend my time talking to the ONE who really loves me. I remember it was Apostle Paul who said the things of this world are nothing but dung. Now I am free of earthly junk or *dung* and I love being free!

If you chose to become one with the Lord you will see help come from places you never expected. Jesus has so many tools to help us and they are all blessings. Jesus will bless you with time for personal prayers, personal thoughts of Him. Jesus will show you His love and Jesus will walk a personal walk with you that is the peace and joy and strength that goes beyond our understanding and it is priceless.

Another big tool to help us walk with the Lord and to live in the love of God when the circumstances of life come against us; is discernment. The simple truth is we need to ask God for His Spirit of discernment. Discernment is hearing the Word of God in your heart. I tell people if you ask God to help you discern His Words of truth then God will bring His truths into your heart.

I believe we all have a truth detector in us somewhere. That is we run everything we hear and see through our very own truth detector to see if there is any truth in what we are hearing and seeing. I believe the Holy Bible is the only book I can read and have what I call my truth detector turned off because the Holy Bible is the truth we are to live by in this world. To me the Holy Bible is the standard for knowing truth, so I can relax while I read it knowing I am reading the truth.

I believe Jesus gave us some real easy ways to discern the truth of His Word. I believe if we want to walk with Jesus we must read these Scriptures and listen for the discernment in them.

1 John 4:1 Beloved, *do not believe every spirit, but test the spirits*, whether they are of God; because many false prophets have gone out into the world.

How do we test the spirits? 1 John 4:2-3 tells us:

1 John 4:2-3 By this you know the Spirit of God: Every spirit that confesses that Jesus Christ has come in the flesh is of God, and every spirit that does not confess that Jesus Christ has come in the flesh is not of God. And this is the *spirit* of the Antichrist, which you have heard was coming, and is now already in the world.

I believe John has made discerning the spirits talking to us really simple. If a person is talking to you and he or she will not confess Jesus Christ has come in the flesh, then they are not of God. I usually never ask people that question. I just know with in minutes of talking to someone if they believe in Jesus Christ or not.

Think about this for a moment; when Jesus was baptized John and Jesus saw and heard Mathew 3:16-17:

Matthew 3:16-17 And Jesus, when he was baptized, went up straightway out of the water: and, lo, the heavens were opened unto him, and he saw the Spirit of God descending like a dove, and lighting upon him: And lo a voice from heaven, saying, This is my beloved Son, in whom I am well pleased.

Through baptism Jesus became the son of God. Our Father declared it from the heavens and the devil wanted to see if Jesus believed it. So the devil came to Jesus and tempted Jesus three times.

Matthew 4:3 And when the tempter came to him, he said, If thou be the Son of God, command that these stones be made bread.

Matthew 4:6 And saith unto him, If thou be the Son of God, cast thyself down: for it is written, He shall give his angels charge concerning thee: and in their hands they shall bear thee up, lest at any time thou dash thy foot against a stone.

72

Matthew 4:9 And saith unto him, All these things will I give thee, if thou wilt fall down and worship me.

The devil is still asking us the same question, 'Do you believe you are a son of God?' Here is another discernment tool: When someone asks you a question that starts with *if* and the question has anything to do with your belief in God, beware of what spirit they have operating in them. If that person is crafty in his questions, doesn't worry just ask them, 'Do you confess Jesus Christ is come in the flesh and is the son of God?' If the person asking says no, then you know the spirit operating in them is not of Jesus Christ.

Jesus even had to ask His own apostles this question.

Matthew 16:15-16 He saith unto them, *But whom say ye that I am?* And Simon Peter answered and said, Thou art the Christ, the Son of the living God.

A precious walk with my Jesus demands a profession of faith like Simon Peter. *Thou art the Christ, the Son of the living God.*

To my amazement, I have friends that will go to Jewish Rabbi's to find some hidden meaning to the Scriptures. It does seem as though the Jewish Rabbi's study the Torah from cover to cover and have access to a lot of information we are not privileged too. One of the things I dearly love about the Jewish faith is their faith is so steadfast in what they believe even thought their faith is not in God.

The first problem I see in going to Jewish Rabbi's for information is. These Rabbis's will not confess Jesus Christ has come in the flesh. The second reason is I believe the Jewish Rabbi's my friends are going to for information, are very slowly and very diplomatically leading my friends into the Jewish religion and away from believing in Jesus Christ. I pray my Messianic friends will be strong in their faith and rooted steadfastly in their faith in Jesus Christ so they will lead the Jewish Rabbi's in to believing in Jesus Christ. After all Jesus said all things are possible and I believe Jesus.

I pray for the Jewish people and all people who do not believe in Jesus Christ to be saved because the word of God says, *"And every spirit that does not confess that Jesus Christ has come in the flesh is not of God, And this is the spirit of the Antichrist."*

You see, there is a spirit of antichrist in the world today. If you do not confess that Jesus Christ has come in the flesh you have a spirit of antichrist in you. Try to think of the spirit of antichrist as any other spirit of sin because being an antichrist is a sin of unbelief. The Word of God says 'Jesus came to lead those who are sick and sinners to repentance.' We have the same commission as Jesus, which is to lead sinners into belief and through belief they will repent.

Mark 2:17 When Jesus heard it, He said to them, "Those who are well have no need of a physician, but those who are sick. I did not come to call the righteous, but sinners, to repentance."

It seems today there are a lot of people who have the spirit of antichrist in them. I only bring this up to help you discern the spirits and to bring an awareness of the need for discerning what spirit is operating in the people you are going to for information. Truthfully I believe we have one source of truth and that source is my Jesus Christ himself. Jesus is our best source because Jesus is truth manifested.

I think I need to clarify something about hearing from the Holy Spirit. I hear form Jesus the best when I am quiet and my spirit is at peace. When I ask God questions and I am in a panic or upset about the circumstances around me, I usually don't have time to listen and in those circumstances I don't seem to hear too well. I hear the answer from God the best in my morning Coffee Time With Jesus. I believe for me the best time to hear from God is first thing in the morning.

Another problem that keeps us from hearing from God is distractions. If I do not hear form Jesus Christ I know I need to fine a quiet place and turn off the distractions of this world. Please stop worrying about the worldly dung we think so much about for it is a distraction. Please think about how much time we waste trying to acquire dung. Please ask God before you go into debt for earthly dung. Please make your relationship with God and what He needs done your first priority everyday and I am sure you will start hearing from my Jesus. You will have the gift of discernment and you will recognize the sinners and the antichrist that are in the world. The best part is you will hear from God and God will tell you how to love them – the sinners into believing in Jesus.

1 John 2:22-23 Who is a liar but he who denies that Jesus is the Christ? He is antichrist who denies the Father and the Son. Whoever denies the Son does not have the Father either; he who acknowledges the Son has the Father also.

These are some real strong powerful words and yet they make discernment really easy. I have faith in hearing the voice of my Jesus because Jesus said I will hear His voice and Jesus said a strangers voice His believers will not follow. A precious walk with my Jesus starts with setting some quiet time aside for listening and receiving the gift of discernment.

I hope you see the discernment in the word of God written in our Holy Bible 'Whoever denies the Son does not have the Father either; he who acknowledges the Son has the Father also.'

Jesus is telling us that we cannot have one without the other. So if someone says they believe in Father God and not Jesus Christ they have neither. You cannot separate one from the other, because they are one. John goes on to say in 2 John 1:17:

2 John 1:7 For many deceivers have gone out into the world who do not confess Jesus Christ as coming in the flesh. This is a deceiver and an antichrist.

Jesus explains through John who the antichrist is and Jesus explains to us the gift of oneness with Jesus and our Father. When we receive the gift of their Holy Spirit we receive one spirit from both the Father and Jesus. Father God and Jesus have one spirit and this is the spirit which is the gift of oneness with them we freely receive from them. I will not try to explain how this works except to say I believe it because Jesus said it. I have been told I am nuts for believing the Word of God and that is okay because I know Father God calls me His son. You see, I am not nuts. I simply believe the word of God that says my Father God adopted me, so I am a Son of God.

In a precious walk with Jesus we simply must believe we are one with Him. Jesus, Father God and I are one! Another way to say this is we simply must believe Jesus and Father God dwell in me and they are alive in me. Therefore, I must love me for I am their creation and they are one with me and they are transforming me into their image and likeness.

Please think for a moment about how much time we parents will spend trying to give our children self esteem by letting them play sports. I believe the attraction to sports, to being the best, to having the best, to more college degrees, all come from a need to have elevated self-esteem. In our quest to give our children the best we seem to be missing or forgetting the only relationship that will give you true value and true worth is intimacy with Jesus. The best we can give our children is oneness with God by knowing and showing them God loves them.

I read the Word and I believe the Word so I know I am one with the Father and the Son because I believe their Holy Spirit dwells in me. Because I believe I have this oneness with Them I also know I have discernment. I cannot even imagine not having discernment while having Them in me. I believe when you receive the Holy Spirit you receive Him completely.

I believe Jesus comes into my life and gives me His whole package. Nothing is held back – I have ALL the gifts of the Holy Spirit in me now. I receive the wholeness of God. Can you imagine God asking you to accept His Holy Spirit into your heart and then only giving you part of Himself. I have an awesome walk with my Lord because I choose to believe He is in me and we are one.

I believe I am protected from deceivers also. Deceivers can be very cunning and very deceiving so you might think that would make them very hard to recognize. Not so. I have Jesus with me and so I know He will protect me because I am loved like my Father God loved his other Son Jesus.

Here is an example of how going to a deceiver can be a problem and how the deceiver very gently tried to lead my

Messianic friends into the law and away from their belief in Jesus Christ.

In my travels I sometimes have the privilege of spending time with some Messianic believers. During one visit the Messianic men were talking about the story in John 8:3. I want to mention my Messianic friends are Christians who believe Jesus Christ is the Son of God. I believe my Messianic friends are trying to please God by keeping the feast and some of the laws of the Old Testament. I have been told a true Messianic is a born and raised Jewish person that converted from Jewish religion to Christianity. The Messianic people I am talking about are Christians who believe in Jesus but want to follow *some* of the laws of Moses.

Okay here is the story I heard my friends talking about.

John 8:3-7 Then the scribes and Pharisees brought to Him a woman caught in adultery. And when they had set her in the midst, they said to Him, "Teacher, this woman was caught in adultery, in the very act. Now Moses, in the law, commanded us that such should be stoned. But what do You say?" This they said, testing Him, that they might have something of which to accuse Him. But Jesus stooped down and wrote on the ground with His finger, as though He did not hear. So when they continued asking Him, He raised Himself up and said to them, "He who is without sin among you, let him throw a stone at her first."

My friends the Messianic men very proudly talked about going to a Jewish Rabbi and asking the Rabbi why did not Jesus stone the adulterous woman to death, after all Jesus was sinless. The Rabbi told these men. Jesus knew the Law of Moses and the Law of Moses states in the case of stoning an adulterous person who is caught in the very act; you must bring both parties and stone them both to death. Therefore Jesus did not want to break the Law of Moses by stoning this woman to death because only the woman was brought to Him.

The Rabbi went on to say, 'You see, if Jesus had stoned the woman to death Jesus would have been breaking the Law of Moses.' The Messianic men in the room where amazed with the Rabbi's answer and with this new insight into the Scriptures.

After hearing their conversation, I very respectfully disagreed with them. I said, "I think you guys missed the whole point of the story. You see, to me Jesus never came to earth to stone anyone. The adulterous woman was seeking love even if the love was momentary and put her in sin. What did Jesus give the woman? Jesus gave her His eternal love of forgiveness. This story was never focus on whether or not Jesus could have stoned her to death or whether or not Jesus was sinless. Simply put the Rabbi's don't care about the forgiveness Jesus gave the woman because the Rabbi's do not believe in Jesus Christ."

The life and walk of Jesus literally proved Jesus came to earth to save souls and Jesus came to earth to show us the love of our Father God. Jesus had His eye on saving her soul and how to bring her into an awareness of His forgiveness. The focus of Jesus was on forgiveness and on giving her a new life, new hope and new freedom form sin. Believe in His forgiveness, believe in Jesus Christ and become the commissioned of Jesus to live the same life and walk the same walk as Jesus Christ walked.

John 8:8-9 And again He stooped down and wrote on the ground. Then those who heard it, being convicted by their conscience, went out one by one, beginning with the oldest even to the last. And Jesus was left alone, and the woman standing in the midst.

Here we see the perfect love of Jesus at work again. Jesus could have condemned the men who brought the woman. Jesus could have said you guys are sinners and worse than this adulterous woman so I think you all should be stoned to death. Again accusing people is not what Jesus came for. Jesus simply put the burden of checking their conscience on themselves. The conviction from my Jesus is so gentle and as you see read in this story the men turned and left one by one.

Here is another discernment tool from my God. Guilt, shame and condemnation are of the devil while gentle conviction is of my Jesus. For me, the gentle love of Jesus and knowing that Jesus loves me gives me the faith to know Jesus will use me to transform more sinners, even antichrist into His perfect love and into believing in Him. This story shows us how Jesus transformed the heart of the adulterous woman and this story is a blue print for how we should walk our precious walk with Jesus.

John 8:10-11 When Jesus had raised Himself up and saw no one but the woman, He said to her, "Woman, where are those accusers of yours? Has no one condemned you?" She said, "No one, Lord." And Jesus said to her, "Neither do I condemn you; go and sin no more."

Can you imagine what that woman felt in her heart at that moment? Jesus gave her His Love, His freedom from the condemnation of sin and Jesus gave her a new belief in His forgiveness. The forgiveness of God is so powerful. Jesus removed a spirit of lust from her and transformed her heart by simply giving her His unconditional love. This is the same love of forgiveness Jesus came to give us. Jesus did not tell her to repent because she was already repenting, accepting the New Life of Jesus, is accepting His goodness and we are told in the word His goodness leads us to repentance.

I believe the sin Jesus came to remove from the Earth is the sin of unbelief. Jesus told this woman to go and sin no more. I believe Jesus was saying to her, 'Daughter you never knew you were loved but now you do know you are loved so go live in the knowledge of knowing you are not condemned but are loved. Never walk in unbelief again and you will *sin no more.*'

I ask my friends; why do you go to Jewish Rabbi's who openly confess Jesus is not the son of God and by their open confession of unbelief in Jesus Christ and His Scriptures that prove they do not have Father God either.

1 John 2:22-23 Who is a liar but he who denies that Jesus is the Christ? He is antichrist who denies the Father and the Son. Whoever denies the Son does not have the Father either; he who acknowledges the Son has the Father also.

This seems so simple to me. I wondered why these messianic men went to Jewish Rabbi's who are professing non believers in Jesus Christ and there by the Rabbi's don't have access to Father God either. Why go to them to get answers to your questions about Jesus Christ the Son of God. I simply don't understand this. Jesus made very clear in John 14:26 that He is the teacher. I believe Jesus, I hear from Jesus and I don't go to Jewish Rabbi's for answers or hidden meaning in the Scripture.

The next morning, I took this same question to Jesus in my Coffee Time With Jesus. Jesus showed me the Rabbi lead these men into the law because the Rabbis believe in the law. The Rabbis don't believe in the love or forgiveness of Jesus Christ because the Rabbi's don't believe in Jesus Christ. When I heard the words of Jesus I said, "Jesus that is so sad." I asked, "Jesus, what I could do to help these Rabbis's come to know you Jesus?" Jesus makes understanding His word simple for me. Jesus answered saying, "Ron, simply be my love to them." And I said, "I will."

Jesus continued, "Ron you believe in me so you will lead anyone who comes to you to me because you believe in me." Jesus said people will lead others into what they believe in. The Rabbi's will lead people into the law and believers in Jesus Christ will lead people into the loving forgiveness of Jesus Christ. I thanked Jesus for making this so simple and so clear to me.

There is one other point I want to make about this story. Notice the penalty for adultery was death by stoning. That seems like a horrible death. The penalty was swift and I assume there was no court battle. I would think the penalty would be enough to stop someone form adultery but it wasn't enough for her. The need for love superseded her fear of the penalty. If she had love in her life she never would have committed the sin of adultery. I think this proves being loved will make keeping the law automatic. Jesus gave her His love!

If you have questions about the stories in the Holy Bible of Jesus Christ, please take your questions to Jesus. Jesus is our source of truth. If you don't seem to get an answer right away, just rest knowing in the future Jesus will bring the answer to you. I do not and will not ever recommend going to anyone who will not profess that Jesus is the Son of God to get answers about my Jesus who is the Son of God.

But if an opportunity comes along, I will gladly go and hang out with Jewish Rabbi's. I will go to a sinner's house to be an example of the love of Jesus to them because I know the love of my Jesus will transform their heart also. We believers must go to these Jewish Rabbi's to give them a chance to see the love of Jesus Christ in action. If we believers of Jesus Christ do not go into the sinner's house, how will the world be transformed? I mean, Jesus came into my house through a believer and Jesus flowed through the believer to start transforming me.

Jesus proved His love for us and I believe that gives Jesus and His Holy Bible preference over the words of men no matter how schooled they are.

When you know Jesus loves you, you will know Jesus will defend you and Jesus is walking with you always.

When you know you are loved by God you will know all things are possible and in the middle of a terrible trial, like a trial that calls for your death like being stoned to death. You will have peace knowing the Creator of the universe is with you to save you. Some people may look for a loop hole in the law such as both parties are not here so we cannot stone her. This is foolishness to a believer who has his trust in Jesus Christ.

We believers need only to stand steadfast in the protection of my Jesus. We will stand steadfast with our faith in my Jesus when you know He is in us and with us and will never leave me or forsake me. I know I am loved by Father God and His Son who are one and their Holy Spirit is dwelling in me and I know the three of us are one. Knowing the three of us are one is now a fact to me. I don't just believe it, I know it! I have received the Holy Spirit of Father God and Jesus into my Spirit and the three of us are one.

I don't know if the woman at the well had faith in Jesus or even knew who He was. But Jesus saved her life and gave her His loving forgiveness. I have faith in Jesus and if I was accused of some crime that called for my death, I bet there would be a lot of *believers* that would tell me, "Don't be stupid. Hire a lawyer to protect yourself." My belief tells me that Romans 8:1 says that there is therefore now no condemnation for those who are in Christ Jesus. I believe Jesus is telling me I don't need a lawyer! Remember in the trial for His life Jesus never hired a lawyer, so why should I?

I also want to say I don't go around accusing Jewish Rabbis of being deceivers. That would be the work of the devil and not me. I believe they are sincere in their belief that Jesus is still to come. I know they are not the only people or religion who will not profess Jesus as the risen Lord. So please don't think for a moment I would approve of believers being mean spirited toward anyone. On the contrary, I believe we are to love them into a relationship with my Jesus. I pray for them to come into a relationship with Jesus and to have a precious walk with my Lord and my Savior. I pray we believers are so steadfast in knowing Jesus loves us we can be the love of Jesus to everyone.

Jesus said it is His goodness that will lead a man to repentance. Believers in Jesus Christ are commissioned by Jesus to be His goodness and His ambassador to everyone everywhere. We are to heal the sick, raise the dead and cast out devils because we are on a precious walk with Jesus by being His loving forgiveness to all. I believe the Holy Spirit will eliminate a lot of confusion in us believers if we simply go to God for the answers to our questions. Hearing from God takes faith and knowing we are hearing from God takes discernment. Knowing we are loved by God is simply receiving His love and knowing God wants to be totally one with us is the peace Jesus told the apostles He would give them.

John 14:27 Peace I leave with you; my peace I give to you. Not as the world gives do I give to you. Let not your hearts be troubled, neither let them be afraid.

Jesus said these words to His apostles and to us. Let us take these words into our heart and receive them as truth, because they are His gift for us. Here again we see the love of Jesus in the details of His care for us. Please receive His peace and your heart will not be troubled or afraid. I will never be troubled or afraid because no man can ever convince me that Jesus didn't exist. No man could ever convince me not to believe Jesus is the Son of God. No man will ever convince me the Holy Spirit of God doesn't live in me. I believe the best way to do the work of the Kingdom – spread the good news is to manifest the kingdom like Jesus did 24/7.

I don't believe in arguing or accusing people of unbelief will change their heart. But being an ambassador of Jesus will allow Jesus to transform the hearts of all people. The best way to be an ambassador for Jesus is to learn of Jesus. Yes, we can walk like Jesus walked, with compassion for our fellow men and see people with the eyes of who created them and who they can be in His image and likeness. Have the mind of Jesus so we can think like Jesus thinks or have the thoughts of Jesus. And yes, we can have the heart of Jesus so we can love like Jesus loves! Jesus will transform your heart, your eyes and your mind but only if you ask Him too. You have a choice and you are choosing every day. Manifest the love of God or manifest the devil of hate.

With the eyes, mind, and heart of Jesus we will walk a precious walk in the peace of knowing Jesus will allow us to speak His Words and Jesus will light our path to the people who have an open heart to listen for His voice! Simply start your day by asking God what are we going to do today and Jesus will handle the rest. That is peace, joy and His love in you manifesting in your peaceful, loving walk with Him.

Discernment

Discernment is so very important in our hearing from God that I want to tell you another story that I think will help us discern.

Jesus in His word tells us to guard our minds by taking all thoughts captive to his Word. Here is a story about a man I met who seemed very confused in His beliefs. I believe if he had asked God for discernment his confusion would leave him completely.

During our conversation this man gave me a book to read. I felt a prompting from the Lord about the book. I knew this man was very confused and I wondered since he had read this book if this book help straighten out his thoughts and bring his thoughts back to God or did it add to the confusion he has in his mind. I opened the book and realized the author used really big words in his book. I would need to look up every third word in a dictionary to try to understand this book.

I went right to Jesus and thank you Jesus for answering my question, "Did this book clear up the confusion of my friend or did it add to his confusion?" After reading only a little of the book I saw some Bible quotes. I felt prompted by Jesus so I read one of the Bible quotes the author had quoted. The Scripture he quoted in his book was John 9:1. It read, "When Jesus and the apostles walked by the man who was blind from birth, Jesus turned to the apostles and ask them who sinned this man or his parents." The moment I read the 'quote' I put the book down and knew I could read no more of it.

I don't personally know the author of this book so I don't know if it was on purpose or not but the author had misquoted this Scripture. Jesus didn't ask the apostles, 'Who sin, this man or his parents?' The apostles asked Jesus who sinned if the man or his parents. The way the author quoted the scripture was confusing, deceitful and very misleading. The big words the author used were the same way to me so I refused to read the book. I go directly to my Jesus and He makes His word. The word of God is very clear and very simple for me to understand.

John 9:1-3 And as Jesus passed by, he saw a man which was blind from his birth. And *his disciples asked him*, saying, Master, who did sin, this man, or his parents, that he was born blind? Jesus answered, Neither hath this man sinned, nor his parents: but that the works of God should be made manifest in him.

The Word of God is very precise and with discernment from God His word becomes very simple to understand. I believe there are people – *deceivers* who have an agenda and will try to confuse the Word of God to us. This is precisely why Jesus and Father God gave us their Holy Spirit to protect us and it is precisely why Jesus gave us His peace when He said no one can pluck us out of His Father's hand.

John 10:27-30 My sheep hear my voice, and I know them, and they follow me: And I give unto them eternal life; and they shall never perish, neither shall any man pluck them out of my hand. My Father, which gave them me, is greater than all; and no man is able to pluck them out of my Father's hand. I and my Father are one.

I walk in an eternal peace of knowing my Father is looking out for me. Jesus said it and I believe it. You too can have His eternal peace if you choose to believe by faith.

Hear is another story of faith. "God whom we serve is able to deliver us."

Please take a moment and read along with me and see how God protected Shadrach and Meshach and Abednego. This story in our Holy Bible is just one of many to show us what true faith in God will do. Jesus delivered them and he will deliver us too.

Daniel 3:1 King Nebuchadnezzar made an image of gold, whose height was sixty cubits and its breadth six cubits. He set it up on the plain of Dura, in the province of Babylon.

The king made everyone worship his idle as a god. There were three men who would not worship the idle. So the king called for them to be thrown into a fire.

Daniel 3:15 Now if you are ready when you hear the sound of the horn, pipe, lyre, trigon, harp, bagpipe, and every kind of music, to fall down and worship the image that I have made, well and good. But if you do not worship, you shall immediately be cast into a burning fiery furnace. And who is the god who will deliver you out of my hands?

Right here we read that King Nebuchadnezzar issued a challenge to believers in our God. "Who is the god who will deliver you out of my hands?" Guess what? They saw the fire and felt the heat and yet their hearts didn't fail. They simply knew their Father would see them through the trial. Read on and see they actually danced in the fire. This is true faith.

Daniel 3:16-17 Shadrach, Meshach, and Abednego answered and said to the king, "O Nebuchadnezzar, we have no need to answer you in this matter. If this be so, our God whom we serve is able to deliver us from the burning fiery furnace, and he will deliver us out of your hand, O king"

Shadrach, Meshach and Abednego knew their God was bigger than king Nebuchadnezzar's fire. They had no fear of what the king could do to them and as you know Our God did deliver them from the fire.

My question is, "Can man build any kind of fire or even a bomb that can harm even one of God's believers?" Please read all of Daniel 3 and see your faith in our God come to life. Notice also that all three stood firm in their faith. They knew they were loved and their name was written in heaven. Isn't it amazing what God will do when we have our faith in Him and by putting our faith in Him we are actually allowing God to build our faith stronger?

I am thinking out loud here. Just for a moment think if these three were searching their past, looking for some sin they might not have repented for our trying to peel off another layer of an onion. They could have asked God 'What did we do to disserve this?' I believe they would have been in doubt instead of faith.

Faith and discernment are very important to hearing from our God. People tell me they want to hear from the Lord but they say they have never heard His voice so how will they know His voice when they do. Jesus gave me this story to tell them.

What if you had a loved one who went to some foreign country and the only way for your loved one to communicate with you was to send you an email. Therefore, every day when you arrive home from work you anxiously open your email to see if your loved one sent you an email. If you have an email from your loved one you naturally open and read it with excitement to hear from your loved one. Please tell me, when you read your loved one's letter, whose voice do you hear as you read?

I believe the love letter – *our Holy Bible* from our Lord Jesus Christ is the same way. Read His love letter like it is a love letter from a loved one because it is! Then as you anxiously read your loved one's love letter you will hear His voice and the excitement in His voice will carry over to you. I believe our Holy Bible is a love letter from heaven and should be treated and cherished with the respect of a love letter.

I met a man in a Bible study a while back. After hearing a couple stories of how my Jesus will use us if we make ourselves available to Him, the man seemed upset. The man proudly proclaimed he had read the Holy Bible from cover to cover 35 times and then he asks me, "How many times have you read the entire bible?" I said, "I haven't read the entire bible yet. You see, when I read my Holy Bible I read to hear from my Jesus. I can read one Scripture and talk to my Jesus for months about that Scripture." I told the man how Jesus and I have Coffee Time together and we sit and talk for hours. I know Jesus was with the apostles more than three years and Jesus hadn't taught them the whole New Testament before He left. I know this is true because the New Testament doesn't end at His death.

I mentioned to him how I read the Scripture in Genesis about Jesus coming in the cool in the day to talk to Adam and how I camped right there with Jesus for months telling Jesus I want you to come to me in the cool of the day everyday so we can talk.

Then someone told me about how in the New Testament where we can have Jesus 24/7 and so I went there. Again, I ask my Jesus for hearing and I believe anyone who asks Jesus for hearing will receive hearing. I believe Jesus is anxious and excited and totally full of joy when we make quite time to hear about His love for us.

Reading the entire Bible is an accomplishment I haven't accomplished yet. I know I will but it will take me years because my Jesus and I talk so much about every detail in His love letter to me. I have asked my Jesus for wisdom that will build the kingdom of God. I believe making yourself available to what God needs done through us His ambassadors is very important to my Jesus. Reading your Holy Bible is very important, for sure. But hearing Jesus talk to you personally through His love letter is precious time with my Jesus and I will never be distracted from this precious time.

Please turn off the distractions of your world and start your day by hearing from my Jesus and very soon the junk of the world will not be so important anymore. Even accomplishments will seem small compared to having intimate time with my Jesus. The best, I mean the *very best accomplishment* I can achieve is to hear from my Jesus every day. Now that's my Jesus and He loves me too.

Want More Faith?

If you are struggling and trying to believe in Jesus, maybe you are looking for a feeling or some miracle to believe in. If your focus is on your healing or getting a feeling you may need to refocus. Jesus said in His word to seek or focus on Him with our whole heart and then all these things will be added.

Matthew 6:33 But seek ye first the kingdom of God, and his righteousness; and all these things shall be added unto you.

The moment we focus on our needs or feelings, we are so easily manipulated. We set ourselves up disappointment and we are actually walking into what I call the danger zone. I know people who go to a church where almost every Sunday the pastor touches people and they are slain in the spirit. I ask them, 'How does that help you?' They said it is hard to explain but you feel so good. The day I went there, I saw that there are a lot of people that were slain in the spirit. But what spirit slain them? I am not really sure.

Please seek ye first the kingdom of God, and his righteousness and all these things shall be added unto you. I don't see where we are told to seek the feeling or our needs, but the kingdom of God. We prove our simple belief in God, when we focus on God. We call on God instead of 911. We live for God instead of dung and God can use you to add hearts to His kingdom. I really don't see how rolling around on the floor laughing or barking like a dog brings glory to God.

Jesus will supply your needs when they line up with His word. You want a precious walk with the Lord? You want faith, you want protection, you want to live without fear, you want to be His ambassador, then simply read the word of God in His Holy Bible for my God has poured out all these blessings and these blessing are all there for us who simply believe like a child!

Listen to the words of Jesus to the apostles after feeding the multitudes with five fishes and some bread.

John 6:26-29 Jesus answered them and said, Verily, verily, I say unto you, Ye seek me, not because ye saw the miracles, but because ye did eat of the loaves, and were filled. Labour not for the meat which perisheth, but for that meat which endureth unto everlasting life, which the Son of man shall give unto you: for him hath God the Father sealed. Then said they unto him, What shall we do, that we might work the works of God? Jesus answered and said unto them, This is the work of God, that ye believe on him whom he hath sent.

Again, we read the questions the apostles ask my Jesus and see the answer is the same answer all through the Bible. BELIEVE ON WHOM HE HATH SENT, JESUS. Like I said, Jesus made everything simple to me. I complete the work of God when I believe on Jesus whom the Father hath sent. I am a child of God and I love being His child. Jesus came as child. Jesus lived childishly in love with His Father and so can we.

We have a battle going on in our heart 24/7. We have choices to make 24/7. If we read our Holy Bible to become Jesus, to follow Jesus, if we surrender our heart to Jesus, we will have peace knowing the battle is the Lord's. Yes, the battle is the Lord's and the battle is for our soul. Believe me Jesus is up for the fight and for He said:

Matthew 18:14 Even so it is not the will of your Father who is in heaven that one of these little ones should perish.

And in Ephesians 6 Jesus tells us the battle is His. All we do is put on the whole armor of God and stand firm.

Ephesians 6:10-11 Finally, my brethren, be strong in the Lord, and in the power of his might. Put on the whole amour of God, that ye may be able to stand against the wiles of the devil.

Some people I know start their day by reading Ephesians 6:10-17 and believe by doing so they are putting on the whole armor of God. If that is where your faith is, then by all means do it. But I don't! I start my day knowing I am loved by God and my God dwells in me and therefore I have it all and I am never without it. I believe I walk in the full armor of God every minute of every day by knowing I am loved by God and by believing in His love for me, I am protected by God. I put the armor on one time and I have lived in the armor just like I got baptized one time and I live baptized.

Actually, by believing God loves me and believing I am one with God the Father and Jesus living in my heart I have received all the gifts of the Holy Spirit in me. I have received all the blessings – peace, joy and all His love and all I need to do to have all this is simply believe God loves me. Now that is simply a precious walk with my Jesus.

Here is a story of faith. Please read about David in 1 Samuel 17 and you will see we don't do the battle. We simply stand firm in the protection our loving Father God that promised us believers who want to walk in faith.

1 Samuel 17:1-4 Now the Philistines gathered together their armies to battle, and were gathered together at Shochoh, which belongeth to Judah, and pitched between Shochoh and Azekah, in Ephesdammim. And Saul and the men of Israel were gathered together, and pitched by the valley of Elah, and set the battle in array against the Philistines. And the Philistines stood on a mountain on the one side, and Israel stood on a mountain on the other side: and there was a valley between them. And there went out a champion out of the camp of the Philistines, named Goliath, of Gath, whose height was six cubits and a span.

We see Goliath was a big man and very intimidating. The whole army of Israel was afraid to fight Goliath. Read on and you will hear about his armor.

1 Samuel 17:9-10 If he be able to fight with me, and to kill me, then will we be your servants: but if I prevail against him, and kill him, then shall ye be our servants, and serve us. And the Philistine said, I defy the armies of Israel this day; give me a man, that we may fight together.

Goliath challenged everyone in the army of Israel to fight him, one on one. The King of Israel did all He could to entice His army men to take up the challenge, the stakes were higher than anyone can imagine and no one would take the challenge.

1 Samuel 17:15-16 But David went and returned from Saul to feed his father's sheep at Bethlehem. And the Philistine drew near morning and evening, and presented himself forty days.

We see the challenge went on for forty days and no one would challenge Goliath. We see David was tending his father's sheep when his father asked him to bring his brothers some food.

1 Samuel 17:17 And Jesse said unto David his son, Take now for thy brethren an ephah of this parched corn, and these ten loaves, and run to the camp to thy brethren

1 Samuel 17:20 And David rose up early in the morning, and left the sheep with a keeper, and took, and went, as Jesse had commanded him; and he came to the trench, as the host was going forth to the fight, and shouted for the battle.

David did as his father had commanded him. David saw Goliath was bigger than big and heard the mouth of Goliath put down our living God. We also know by His words and actions David knew God was real and living.

1 Samuel 17:26 And David spake to the men that stood by him, saying, What shall be done to the man that killeth this Philistine, and taketh away the reproach from Israel? for who is this uncircumcised Philistine, that he should defy the armies of the living God?

David wanted to know why all the army of Israel was afraid. The whole army of Israel had the same opportunity to know God, to learn of God and to be a believer in God, just as David believed. David starts building the faith of Saul.

1 Samuel 17:32-35 And David said to Saul, Let no man's heart fail because of him; thy servant will go and fight with this Philistine. And Saul said to David, Thou art not able to go against this Philistine to fight with him: for thou art but a youth, and he a man of war from his youth. And David said unto Saul, Thy servant kept his father's sheep, and there came a lion, and a bear, and took a lamb out of the flock: And I went out after him, and smote him, and delivered it out of his mouth: and when he arose against me, I caught him by his beard, and smote him, and slew him.

Saul was right. David was a youth. I am told David was about fourteen years old and very skinny little boy. David pleaded to fight by telling Saul about the lion and the bear.

1 Samuel 17:36-37 Thy servant slew both the lion and the bear: and this uncircumcised Philistine shall be as one of them, seeing he hath defied the armies of the living God. David said moreover, The LORD that delivered me out of the paw of the lion, and out of the paw of the bear, he will deliver me out of the hand of this Philistine. And Saul said unto David, Go, and the LORD be with thee.

David pleaded his case and won. Saul must have seen something in David he didn't see in any of his army men. The something he saw was courage that came from faith in God.

1 Samuel 17:38-39 And Saul armed David with his armour, and he put an helmet of brass upon his head; also he armed him with a coat of mail. And David girded his sword upon his armour, and he assayed to go; for he had not proved it. And David said unto Saul, I cannot go with these; for I have not proved them. And David put them off him.

Saul wanted to protect David with physical armor but the armor was for men not youths and David said I cannot go with these; for I have not proved *them*. And David put them off him.

I believe David had all his trust and faith in His God. The Kings physical armor meant nothing to him and I am told, with the physical armor on him, David could hardly move. David's armor was spiritual and invisible but he had it on because David knew he was loved by God. Yes here again we see our armor is knowing we are loved by God.

1 Samuel 17:42-43 And when the Philistine looked about, and saw David, he disdained him: for he was but a youth, and ruddy, and of a fair countenance. And the Philistine said unto David, Am I a dog, that thou comest to me with staves? And the Philistine cursed David by his gods.

When Goliath saw a youth came out to fight him, he was upset and cursed our living God. Instead of being afraid, David told big old Goliath what his God can do through a man of faith.

1 Samuel 17:46-47 This day will the LORD deliver thee into mine hand; and I will smite thee, and take thine head from thee; and I will give the carcases of the host of the Philistines this day unto the fowls of the air, and to the wild beasts of the earth; that all the earth may know that there is a God in Israel. And all this assembly shall know that the LORD saveth not with sword and spear: *for the battle is the LORD'S, and he will give you into our hands.*

Right here we read why David won against the giant Goliath. David won because he believed His God was bigger, more capable, more powerful, then any man, no matter how big Goliath was. David knew in his heart. His God loved Him and David knew the love of His God was his armor. David knew the fight was His Lord's for he said so and David knew His living God would triumph.

Notice David didn't fast for three days, or pray and ask, 'God, is this your will?' No. David had a living relationship with a living God and it was truly his relationship with God that gave David the boldness, the faith and the truth of what a loving God will do. My God will move mountains for me, will yours?

1 Samuel 17:48-50 And it came to pass, when the Philistine arose, and came and drew nigh to meet David, that David hasted, and ran toward the army to meet the Philistine. And David put his hand in his bag, and took thence a stone, and slang it, and smote the Philistine in his forehead, that the stone sunk into his forehead; and he fell upon his face to the earth. So David prevailed over the Philistine with a sling and with a stone, and smote the Philistine, and slew him; but there was no sword in the hand of David.

I have often wondered if David even aimed the stone. In my heart I don't believe he aimed the stone. I believe he simply felt prompted and did what he was prompted to do. I believe this because most of the promptings I get make no sense to my mind but if I act on the prompting I see a miracle.

1 Samuel 17:51 Therefore David ran, and stood upon the Philistine, and took his sword, and drew it out of the sheath thereof, and slew him, and cut off his head therewith. And when the Philistines saw their champion was dead, they fled.

Here we see fear entered the hearts of the Philistines the moment big old Goliath died. Also, here we see when faith is present in us. Our faith is also contagious for the fear of the Israelites left the minute they saw little David slay Goliath.

1 Samuel 17:52-58 And the men of Israel and of Judah arose, and shouted, and pursued the Philistines, until thou come to the valley, and to the gates of Ekron. And the wounded of the Philistines fell down by the way to Shaaraim, even unto Gath, and unto Ekron. And the children of Israel returned from chasing after the Philistines, and they spoiled their tents. And David took the head of the Philistine, and brought it to Jerusalem; but he put his armour in his tent. And when Saul saw David go forth against the Philistine, he said unto Abner, the captain of the host, Abner, whose son is this youth? And Abner said, As thy soul liveth, O king, I cannot tell. And the king said, Enquire thou whose son the stripling is. And as David returned from the slaughter of the Philistine, Abner took him, and brought him before Saul with the head of the Philistine in his hand. And Saul said to him, Whose son art thou, thou young man? And David answered, I am the son of thy servant Jesse the Bethlehemite.

We too can have the faith of David and we too can kill the giants in our life with simple faith in our living God. Today we to can proclaim our victory and stand stead fast knowing we don't need earthly armor; all we need is just simple faith in our living God.

1 Samuel 17:47 and that all this assembly may know that the LORD saves not with sword and spear. *For the battle is the LORD's, and he will give you into our hand.*

David stood strong. Shadrach and his friends stood strong. Jesus stood strong in His trial. Look at the examples we have in our Holy Bible. Every example points to the fact they knew they were loved by God and His love for them is what would give them the strength to willing face whatever the enemy puts in their path. Do you believe you are loved or not? I really think faith like that of David will not become real to us if we are watching television or doing what we want to please our self or if we are too busy with whatever your distraction is.

Please turn of the distractions and get into the life of Jesus and ask Jesus to let you become His life. Faith is ours for the asking but we must choose to be hearing also. I know I have heard the voice of Jesus while in a noise place so I know Jesus will talk to me where ever I am. But I believe Jesus would much rather talk to me while I am quietly, willingly, listening for Him and to Him.

Speaking of noises and distractions and hearing from God, a couple days ago I was invited to a restaurant called Roasters. The place is nothing but noise. There are televisions everywhere and some stupid football game was on that everybody was screaming about. I had a good meal but talking with my friends was so hard and I wondered if my friends could hear what I was talking about.

After our meal, I walked to my car and just sat quietly for a moment. I thought, 'Dear Jesus is that what it is like for You to talk to us? I was so glad to get out of there.' I wondered if Jesus is waiting for us to get out of our noisy place in life. It was just too much noise for my ears and so many distractions for my eyes. Then I thought, I wonder if Jesus was thinking the same thing, when we fill our life with noise and distractions. I wonder if Jesus is waiting patiently for us to go somewhere quiet and listen.

Jesus always went off to the mountains and or desert to have quiet time with His Dad. Both places are quiet. Jesus is our example, and Jesus is waiting to have quiet time with us. You don't need a vacation in the mountains to have quiet time with my Jesus, but if you have the time and resources, then do it.

Want Some More Good News?

We are one with Jesus and Father God!

Do you believe we are one with the Lord? We simply must believe being one with the Lord in us is possible. David believed he was one with our Lord. We have the advantage of being able to read the Word of God freely in this world. Read these Scriptures and you too will know you were born to be one with my Jesus.

John 17:22 And the glory which thou gavest me I have given them; that they may be one, even as we are one:

All through our Holy Bible we have examples of the glory Jesus gave us for simply believing we can be one with Him. We bring Glory to God when we believe *that they may be one, even as we are one*. You see the goal. We are to be one with Father God just as Father God and Jesus are one in each other. We are one with them if we simply let them into our heart. Yes, the power and glory of Jesus Christ are given to us through Jesus to bring Glory to Jesus Christ. I believe I am one with them. The love of Father God is one with Jesus and now they are one with me because I believe their word. I pray you do too.

John 17:23 I in them, and thou in me, that they may be made perfect in one; and that the world may know that thou hast sent me, and hast loved them, as thou hast loved me.

Listen to the words Jesus chose. *'I in them'* meaning He is in us, Jesus in us as God the Father is in Jesus. Jesus wants us to be perfectly in one with Him and Jesus wants the world to know, that God the Father sent Him and intern Jesus has sent us. When we believe we are loved by God we will glorify God by being the love of God just as Jesus believed He was the love of God. The world will know us by His love. We will be defined by His love. I pray the world comes to know His love through His love in me. I simply will not be defined by anything else especially a man-made denomination. I have set my will to only be defined by a declaration of His manifested love in me.

I want to share this for a moment. I believe this story shows us how through prayer we can be the love of Jesus to others. I have had the great honor to meet James Knabe family. I could tell you a lot of stories about them. So here is one: Their son Jay is 14 years old and was interviewed about his relation to a football quarterback on the Hawks team. The team went 12 and 0 this year. The quarterback is now pretty famous and when he was asks about his success he contributed it to the prayers Jay says for him.

So a news reporter called Jay for an interview. At the end of the interview Jay was asked, "What denomination are you from?" I believe Jay's answer was perfect. Jay said, "Sir, there are no denominations in heaven. Only truth: God's truth. All that other stuff gets washed away." To meet the Knabe family, go to *desertrainblog.com*.

Yes, the world will see in us the love Jesus modeled and the world should see the life Jesus lived for us in us, so we can share His love just as He shared His Father's love with us throughout His life. We can and should model His perfect love throughout our life by studying His life not to quote it but to become it. I believe we can become His love, do you? Jesus said all things are possible to those that believe and I believe and I pray you do too.

Do you believe we can be perfect in His love? I believe we can be perfect when we trust Him to give us His heart, His eyes, and His mind. Yes we may be made perfect in one with God, just as Father God sent His Son and loved Jesus and made Him the perfect Son. Father God wants to make us His perfect son's through his love for us if we simply believe He will.

Father God loves us like He loved His Son Jesus perfectly. Thinking we can be perfect might sound like a stretch but being perfect is possible or God would not have told us so. Yes, we can be made perfect by seeking God with all our heart and believing

He will perfect His love in us. So being perfect is possible. I believe that a precious walk with my Jesus is possible, do you?

Please read these Scriptures and listen as Jesus prays to His Father for his apostles and us:

John 17:20 I'm not praying only for them. *I'm also praying for those who will believe in me through their message.*

Here we see we are commissioned to carry on the message! Please just believe. It really is simple if we let Jesus give us the message. When we remove earthly junk and our earthly thinking we will hear from God and know the message. Forget religion and simply ask God to transform you into His image and likeness.

John 17:21 I pray that all of these people continue to have unity in the way that you, Father, are in me and I am in you. I pray that they may be united with us so that the world will believe that you have sent me.

Here we see the message we are to carry to the world. We are united with the Father through the Son *so that the world will BELIEVE that you Father have sent me.* I believe the whole New Testament is about believing Jesus is the Son of God and believing in the changes Jesus gave us in the new covenant. To be a child of God, to walk a Godly walk, is to simply believe that as Father God sent His son Jesus, Father God sends us. Jesus had the Father's words and so do we. With a child-like faith in God you will believe God and have no fear for God will give you the words and you will speak them boldly.

John 17:22 *I have given them the glory that you gave me.* I did this so that they are united in the same way we are.

Jesus is the ultimate giver of gifts and the most unselfish person to ever walk this earth. Come on please think about this: Jesus gives us all the gifts of the Holy Spirit, Jesus gives us His perfect love, His joy, His peace, His hope, His life and now we see Jesus shares with us His glory and His Father. There simply is nothing to be held back. Please join the Jesus team and become a spoke person for God.

A precious walk with my Jesus is walking as a Son of God, by believing you are a son of God. Even the Glory of God is shared with us believers. Jesus tells us why, "I did this so that they are united in the same way we are." Nothing is held back! Being united is boldness you never knew before, it is peace beyond our understanding, and it is loving others like we never loved before.

How can we not love someone so giving? You want to walk with my Jesus, you want Him to call you by name, and you want to live knowing your name is written in heaven, you want to follow Jesus Christ on His narrow path. You want to be His love to everyone you meet. You can when you simply believe you can because He said we believers can and Jesus said all things are possible to those who believe. We are united exactly the same way Jesus the man was united with our Father God. I believe it by faith in God.

I mentioned the Knabe family earlier. They have six children and live in a camper on the road. On the surface that makes them kind of special. I know their specialness comes from their relationship with God who shines through them. You will see the love and the trust in God the moment you meet them. I believe the voice of God comes through their children; if you want some heaven on earth you don't have to do something special like live in a camper with six children. Simply ask God for His eyes and His heart and His mind and Jesus will gladly gift them to you. The gifts of God will become evident to everyone you meet. I believe the Knabe family has the gifts of God because I see them flowing and it is obvious they walk a precious walk with the Lord.

To live in a camper with six children makes the Knabe family unique. Being unique does not make them special to God. I know a lot of families that try to be unique or different by outward appearances or some unique material possession. When I first saw them, I knew immediately something was different. After asking Jesus one morning, He said you see my presence in them. I thank you Jesus for your eyes, your mind and your heart of love, I see in them.

John 17:23 I am in them, and you are in me. So they are completely united. In this way the world knows that you have sent me and that you have loved them in the same way you have loved me.

Listen to the Words of my Jesus. Read them over and over. Jesus cannot make His intensions any clearer. Jesus wants for us to experience His love so completely we are for sure and without any doubt His children. Jesus wants us to know our Father loves us in the same way our Father loves Jesus. We are co-heirs, Jesus said so!

Here Jesus prays for us. Listen to words Jesus chose. Jesus knows the power in prayer. Please listen with your heart to the words from the heart of my Jesus.

John 17:24-26 "Father, I want those you have given to me to be with me, to be where I am. I want them to see my glory, which you gave me because you loved me before the world was made. Righteous Father, the world didn't know you. Yet, I knew you, and these disciples have known that you sent me. I have made your name known to them, and *I will make it known so that the love you have for me will be in them and I will be in them.*"

Do you hear the heart of God and Jesus in the prayer my Jesus said for us? I believe Jesus wants us to know we can and will be one with Him if we ask Him into our heart. The heart of God is for us to know we are loved just as much as Father God loved His Son, Jesus. There was nothing our Father God didn't do for Jesus so we can know there is nothing our Father God won't do for us. I hear people say *if it is His will*. Well here is the will of our Father God and Jesus. If you need to understand His will please read these scriptures again.

Jesus wants us to be with Him and to know our righteous Father. Jesus came to make known to us. The love of the righteous Father has for us. I just don't know a better way to say it. We are to make known the love of the Father to everyone also. We have the same commission Jesus had. We are here to do the work of the kingdom by being the kingdom by manifesting the kingdom of God to everyone.

Also in these Scriptures Jesus used the word *united* and *completely united* to describe how we can become one with Him if we simply believe in His love for us. Our belief is so important to my Jesus that Jesus actually prays for us to believe. Please read John 17:20 to 17:26 again. I believe this proves Jesus knew the power in prayer and was teaching us how to pray. When I hear people pray for financial blessings, I cringe and I pray for them to come to know the love of God is so much more then momentary money.

Notice we must believe in His love for us. For when we believe in His love for us we are being transformed into His image and likeness and His love for us is the rock we stand on and unite on! Being the love of God to others just as Jesus was the love of God to others is the goal of our heavenly Father. I believe I have been made one with them, do you?

These Scriptures give us another discerning tool. We have learned a better way to pray, we have learned the ways of Jesus should be our ways. Jesus was not a coward and we should never be cowards when we know Jesus is in us. If we feel cowardly we are not hearing form Jesus. We should choose our words like Jesus chose His – by asking Jesus for His words. If our words would sound funny or stupid coming from Jesus they should sound funny or stupid coming from us.

How Your Walk Wins Hearts to Jesus

I hear people argue over what they perceive His Holy Bible to say. My heart is so saddened when I hear people argue over the Words of my Jesus. I mean, Jesus gave us a channel or a connection directly to Him. Jesus said in John 14:26:

John 14:26 However, the helper, the Holy Spirit, whom the Father will send in my name, will teach you everything. He will remind you of everything that I have ever told you.

Yes, I believe Jesus is still our Teacher, Comforter, and Savior. But instead of arguing over what we think His Word says we can go directly to our teacher and hear directly from the teacher of teachers what His words are for us today. Notice in the Holy Bible, when the apostles had a question they went directly to Jesus. We have the same opportunity to go directly to Jesus every second of everyday. This is the good news, we can go directly to God and we will hear from God. Jesus died to give us this open communication. Jesus in His word says he is no respecter of persons and I believe Jesus. I have open communication with my Jesus everyday just like the apostles.

I know we have a lot of denominations out there and they split hairs over what they think the Holy Bible says. I personally have never seen anyone have a heart change while arguing; but if you give of yourself and show them the love of Jesus you will see hearts transformed and these transformed hearts will not go back to the their old ways. Die to yourself to be transformed by my teacher and your teacher Jesus Christ who is in love with you will lead us into all truth. Now that is the road to perfection! I believe do you?

I believe dying to our self is another great way to bring someone to the Lord. Yesterday, I left a campground so I could go where I believed I was prompted to go. The drive was over 200 miles and there was not one rest area along the way. When I was 20 miles from the campground the road I needed to be on was closed for reconstruction. My GPS kept trying to get me back to the closed road. I thank God I have a GPS system. By the time I arrived at the campground I was exhausted and wanted to eat and just go to sleep. The people I was supposed to meet were running late so we could not meet for dinner until eight PM. I wanted to excuse myself and go to sleep in my camper.

Instead, I meet the couple at eight and it was obvious something was wrong. They didn't confide in me what was wrong but Jesus prompted me to tell some stories. I was talking as they ate their dinner so I had the waiter box my dinner, to eat back at the camper. When we walked out of the restaurant the couple asks to come to my camper so we could spend some more time together.

We did and Jesus again had me tell some more stories. By the end of the night they seemed to have the heaviness lifted and were smiling and laughing. It was truly exciting to see Jesus lift their spirits so fast. After they left my camper I just marveled at what Jesus had done and thanked Him for giving me His strength to carry on that night.

The next day in my Coffee Time With Jesus, Jesus let me know He was pleased with me for dying to myself. I had such a joy in my heart when that couple left because they seemed to have a renewed focus on my Jesus again. I ate my dinner from last night and it was still very tasty. Thank you Jesus, I love you too! Jesus is my teacher and now after years of hating school. I love being in school and I love being the teacher's pet. I love being loved by my teacher. I believe in the love of God, do you? Now that's a transformation.

Our walk will transform hearts to the Lord when we lay down our life and do what we are prompted to do. Yes, laying down your life can be as simple as putting your tiredness aside to do what you are prompted to do and the reward is seeing your friends hearts lifted. Jesus is so gentle.

While on a precious walk with Jesus, you will encounter people of different denominations. As we walk are walk with Jesus we will be tempted to align ourselves to a denomination. I wonder sometimes about all these 'Christian' denominations we have here on earth. I wonder what God thinks about when He sees all the different denominations. Are His people glorifying God or building their own denomination? What happened to seek ye first the kingdom of God?

It seems some people are more pleased about someone becoming or declaring their belief in their denomination instead of receiving the Joy of the Lord. There is no strength in you declaring a denomination no matter how big that denomination is. Our strength, our joy comes from a relationship with my Jesus. Jesus tells us to focus on Him and what He needs us to do today. Please focus on Jesus and Jesus will flow through you to bring souls into relationship with Jesus. We are commissioned to manifest the kingdom of Jesus, not the kingdom of your denomination.

I really cannot imagine Father God and Jesus being pleased with all these denominations we have started here on Earth. I personally see them as dividing not uniting, yet here in John we see how to Glorify God by becoming one with Him perfectly through simply believing in the power of the love Jesus and Father God have for us. To me all the division or arguing about these denominations prove we are trying to love God in our own strength and we are trying to love God instead of letting the love of God transform us. We need to realize our true strength comes from knowing the love God has for us.

I thank God for allowing me to talk in churches of many different denominations. Although they all have some differences in their beliefs, I believe we are not nearly as far apart as some might think. I believe in the Good News of Jesus and the power in the love of Jesus Christ. I believe His love is totally capable of uniting these churches and when the trial comes, we Christians will definitely unite. My point is even if you declare a denomination to belong to, my teacher – my Jesus is willing and capable of using you.

Here is a realistic question that seems to come up about hearing from God. I am told we have over 800 different Baptist churches and I am pretty sure they all think they are right. There are so many different Christian churches it seems there is a church for everyone. The question is, "Are all these people hearing from God? And if so does that make them right?" I believe I am hearing from God while writing this book, so does that make me right? Some people tell me they only deal in facts. So factually they believe they are right.

I have talked a lot in this book about discernment and how important it is. I have talked a lot about what God asks us to do before He ascended into heaven. I don't see anywhere in the Bible we are to pick and choose what Scriptures to believe in. I do see simple beliefs like my sheep hear my voice, Jesus is our teacher, and the Holy Spirit of truth dwells in us if we let Him. These simple beliefs make me a vessel for the Lord.

I want you to know there are scriptures I read that I don't have any idea what my Jesus is telling me in them. I have full faith if I need to know their meaning Jesus will tell me. I believe I am on a need to know bases with my Jesus. I fear not, for I know I have Jesus living in me and my faith is in Him not my knowledge. Again my faith in Jesus makes my life simple and I believe I might sound childish to you but I have Jesus and he protects me.

If I talk to someone and they tell me they are hearing from Jesus and in my spirit I hear the complete opposite I do not argue with them. I go right to my Jesus. I don't believe in arguing. I listen for His voice and if I hear I speak and if I don't hear I don't speak. I know by faith Jesus is speaking to them through His spirit.

I remember a story where a friend came into my camper and downloaded for an hour and the whole time I was asking God what to say to her. It seemed she was way more advanced in her Bible knowledge then I and she was definitely holding unforgiveness toward her husband. I didn't hear anything from God so I was just listened but I had absolutely no comment. She screamed at me as she slammed the door on my camper saying, "You men are so stupid! You are all alike!"

Two days later she came back to my camper and told me, "Two days ago I was mad. I wanted to argue with you so bad that night but for some reason you said nothing. She told me how my silence drove her nuts and when she went back to her camper she sat down and finally turned to God and said God please help me, this is driving me nuts, no one understands me and God opened my heart to hear Him." Thank You Jesus for discernment to know when to talk and when to be quiet. I thank you Jesus for showing me in your word you never argue.

I know Jesus never argued. Arguing or debating is a tactic of the devil. To argue means someone is right and someone else is wrong. I know arguing doesn't change the heart but I know the one who can and He will use me to change the heart of others. My faith is not in me and my ability to argue. My faith is not in my Bible knowledge. My faith is in hearing from the one who loves me and I know my Jesus will never lead me astray. My faith has never led me to believe I can change anyone's heart but with Jesus flowing through me. Well, I know now all things are possible. Sometimes being quiet can lead someone to the Lord.

I believe we are to focus on Jesus and what He needs done today because we will win when we simply focus on Jesus. Here is a short story of how focusing on Jesus solved a problem, made the devil flee and took away pain:

Last spring, I was asked to share some stories on Sunday morning in a church. The night before I was to speak I went to the home of some friends for dinner. This nice couple gave me a gift of some organic coffee. I told them I would have the organic coffee in my coffee pot in the morning while having my Coffee Time With Jesus.

The next morning I drank a cup of this wonderful coffee and had no idea how strong it was. My hands started shaking, my stomach went nuts. I quickly drank milk and had two bottles of water to drink on the way to church. At church they promptly put a microphone on my ear. During the third song I ran for the bathroom again and tried to relieve the pain in my stomach. I was alone in the bathroom, so I cried out loud to the Lord to help me. When I walked into church again it seemed a whole lot of people turned to look at me. I thought please God tell me that microphone wasn't on. Jesus saved me again; the microphone was not on, thank you Jesus.

Within seconds I was in front of the whole congregation and my stomach was literally full of shooting pains. The pastor introduced me. I walked to the podium and started speaking. The pastor had me talking for almost two hours. The whole time I had no pain whatsoever. Really, it was the fastest two hours of my life. The rest of the day went great. Meet a lot of people and shared the Good News with everyone and gave away a lot of Jenny's books. After the busy day, I got in my car to head back to my camper for the night and finally I had time to talk to my Jesus.

I started thanking Jesus for the taking all my pain the second I stepped up to podium. As I thanked Him I heard His voice in my heart. Jesus asked, "What did you do when you stepped to the podium?" I replied, "I asked you Jesus. What do you want to say?" Then Jesus said, "No Ron, I am not asking what did you say when you got to the podium, but what did you do?" I thought quietly for a moment and all of a sudden I had my answer. I said, "Jesus I focused on You." And wow, immediately my problem – the stomach pain and gas pain went away. Now that's my Jesus!

When we focus on the problem we are defeated. When we focus on God, especially focusing on the fact God hears us and has an answer for us because He loves us, then we win. Our focus really needs to be on God and what He needs done. So declare a denomination if you want but keep your focus on God and don't be limited by your choice. Remember, believers are His light to the world and Jesus has you in your denomination for a real good reason. You are the light in your denomination.

Here is a short story about discernment. A while ago, some friends said their pastor was preaching on John 8 where the Pharisees brought the adulterous woman to Jesus in the temple. The preacher gave his whole sermon on *What Jesus Wrote on the Ground?*

John 8:6 This they said, tempting him, that they might have to accuse him. But Jesus stooped down, and with his finger wrote on the ground, as though he heard them not.

The preacher talked for an hour and a half about how he had researched and found what the big name philosophers in Bible studies think Jesus wrote on the ground. My friends told me what their preacher had found out and how interesting his findings were. I guess I didn't look too impressed and so they ask me if I thought his findings were interesting. I told them no. For me the findings were all just conjecture and I believe if what Jesus wrote on the ground was important Jesus would have told us in His Holy Bible what He wrote on the floor of the temple. Jesus did not tell us so I am not interested in spending my time trying to find out what Jesus didn't tell us.

Again, the stories in our Holy Bible are not there to see how interesting we can make them, but really they are to build our faith. I believe learning what Jesus actually did is how we can learn to trust Father God the way Jesus trusted our Father. To me, interesting is another word I use to discern. Jesus is more than interesting. Jesus is truth and Jesus is love. I want Jesus in my heart so I have His truth and His love in me. I want to be the love of Jesus to my friends and love is more than interesting.

Our walk is to be an action of love.

I loved my wife Jenny with all my heart but I did not have any joy or peace in loving her until I knew she loved me. My love for Jenny actually made me uneasy and nervous. I spent hours thinking about how to please her and make her love me. I remember my focus was on Jenny and how to make myself loveable to her.

The moment Jenny revealed her love for me I thought could have moved the mountains myself. When I knew in my heart Jenny loved me, I received great joy and peace. I could hardly wait until we married. Our love and joy for each other gave us both peace.

How did Jenny know I loved her or how did I know Jenny loved me. Jenny could have sung to me every Sunday about how much she loved me. Jenny could have told me she loved me everyday and none of her singing or talking would prove to me how much she loved me until Jenny proved her love with actions of love. For me, actions of love are. Jenny and I thought about each other always. We never had to repeat ourselves because we were listening to each other. Well, I must admit Jenny was a lot better than me at listening, Jenny knew my faults and never used them against me but instead she helped me improve. Jenny set time aside to spend with me, and Jenny made being with me her priority. Jenny even prayed for me to be who God created me to be. These are actions of love that prove your love and we did them for each other.

Now I believe Jesus loves me. I believe Jesus and Father God receive great joy from knowing I choose to believe in their love for me. I believe Jesus and Father God call me by name. Yes, I know they love me and yes they know I love them by the works of faith I do, actions of love I do. I know they make listening to me their priority and I do the same. If you will make them your priority, listen with discernment, set aside quiet time to be with them, they will respond with love beyond your understanding.

Jesus proved His love for us with action. He healed, He cast out devils, He raised the dead but more then all those combined is His gift of His loving forgiveness to us. I tell everyone Jesus is my best friend. I sing about how much I love Jesus and these are just words and they are easy to say, especially while around others singing on Sunday morning. I ask you, "Do you sing as you are walking down the street where nonbelievers can hear you?" I thank you God for giving me the ability to prove my belief Jesus loves me; by becoming His love to everyone I meet.

For example, I believe true love is more than say, feeding the hungry... I believe true love is being the love of Jesus to the hungry. Love is sitting down with them as they eat and listening to their needs and taking the time to love on them. I believe that is how we can give someone the desire to know God, I don't think of myself as a teacher but more importantly a demonstrator of His love. When we demonstrate His love we give people the desire to know Him more. For it is the demonstration of His powerful love that opens hearts and allows my Jesus to transform their heart.

Remember we let the love of Jesus flow as we plant seeds of His love. Remember God said He will bring the increase. The best farmer in the world can only plant seeds. But if the seeds do not grow the farmer will be puzzled, the scientist will be puzzled, but we believers won't be puzzled because we know only God can bring an increase. While we are on our walk we are to plant the seeds of God's love and God will bring the increase.

To me the only thing worth living for is the faith that we can be transformed into Sons of God. I believe I am a son of God. Jesus believed He was the son of God. Everyone knew Jesus healed the sick, raised the dead, cast out devils, and forgave sins but calling Himself a son of God got Him crucified. Believing and declaring you are a Son of God boldly to the world and being the love of Jesus to the world is what sets us apart and makes us what Jesus called a peculiar people. I love being a peculiar person of God. Being adopted into the family of Jesus is knowing I am loved by Jesus because He and I choose each other and I know His love is forever.

Because of our mutual adoption I have the privilege to walk in the precious love of Jesus and to share His love to everyone I meet. The love of Father God in Jesus is what gave Jesus the super human strength to carry His cross and will give us the super human strength to carry our cross. All through life we receive His never ending love. His love in us is what we are to give away to everyone we meet. This is Joy beyond our understanding.

This Joy of the Lord will not come from declaring and believing in a denomination. We are to simply believe and follow in Jesus for Jesus said come follow me. Jesus made believers out of fishermen and tax collectors and Jesus transformed them into bold Sons of God. This boldness came into them when Jesus breathed new life into them.

Notice the apostles had walked and talked to Jesus the man for three years, so the apostles knew of Jesus and they were friends of Jesus and had witness the miracles of Jesus. They had seen everything Jesus did and yet had no courage to declare their friendship to Jesus at the time of His death. Friends, we need to know we are adopted into the family of Father God to receive this boldness. Please get baptized by water and the Spirit of my Father God. But you must believe you received the Holy Spirit too receive Him into your heart. The only thing you give up is earthly junk or dung and the fear of dying.

Think about this: a robot can sing in church 24/7 'We worship you, we worship you we love you we love you' over and over. A robot can say I love you over and over 24/7 and none of this would be fellowshipping or worshiping with God and none of this would prove you have chosen to obey, follow, love and glorify

God. Thank God we are not robots. We have life and choices to make daily. Truthfully the only way to glorify God is through our believing in His love for us. We prove our beliefs by works of faith. Yes works of faith are more than singing on Sunday morning or keeping the feast. I believe faith works by love and love flows through us by faith.

God gave us a choice and the choice is we must choose to understand God loves us in our circumstance or we are choosing to believe in the devil. The moment you say 'Why is this happening?' or 'Where are you Lord?' we are declaring how small our belief in God is. Our questions and our prayers usually declare how small or how big our belief is in our Lord. Our whole life is about choices, so I guess you could say we are still choosing to eat or not to eat of the tree of knowledge of Good and evil every time we make a choice. The choice is, do we believe in God's love for us or not? Have we denied ourselves or not? Are we following or not? Are we simply singing like robots or not?

In the word, we see Jesus said My Father God desires fellowship. Originally, God made angels and somewhere along the way Lucifer decided he could be a god to himself. He betrayed the love and the trust God had in him and God kicked him out of heaven.

Luke 10:18 And he (Jesus) said unto them, I beheld Satan as lightning fall from heaven.

I believe we can be born again. We can become partakers in the image and likeness of God. The Word says so and I believe! I believe we have been given the greatest gift possible and that is a desire for fellowship with Jesus. As followers of Jesus we will have a great desire to please others and see them joyful also. Jesus said we can bring or live in heaven while on Earth. We were created innocent; we lived naked in a garden and had no shame. I believe we are given our innocence back when we are born again. I know for a fact there is no shame in following Jesus so if you have any shame in your heart, the shame never came from Jesus. Remember Jesus is about the future and not the past. Seek ye first the kingdom of God and not the past.

John 3:17-18 For God did not send His Son into the world to condemn the world, but that the world through Him might be saved. "He who believes in Him is not condemned; but he who does not believe is condemned already, because he has not believed in the name of the only begotten Son of God.

Jesus tells us He did not come to condemn us. The sins of our past condemn us. Only the devil will bring up the sins of your past. John 3:18 says 'He who believes in God is not condemned, but he who does not believe is condemned already, because he has not believed in the name of Jesus the only begotten Son of God.' To me, this is simple. The opposite of condemnation is forgiveness. Love is forgiveness. Jesus is loving us by forgiving us. I believe in Jesus and my belief in Jesus leads me into repentance for my sins. I don't try to figure Him out and come up with religion. I just simply believe and my life becomes a peaceful, joyful walk knowing I am loved by Jesus and his love makes me desire repentance. I love being (forgiven) by Jesus and I love desiring my Jesus so much that I can deny myself.

When Adam sinned by listening to the devil, the selfish desires of the devil entered into Adam's heart and from that time on we have had to make choices as to who we are listening too. The desire I am talking about is the desire to be a God unto you. This desire is what got Satan kicked out of heaven and it is the desire to be a god to ourselves that makes us try to explain things of the Earth through science like the creation of the world. Wanting to be a god to yourself through knowledge will probably get you condemned. I thank you Jesus; you are the judge not me.

Genesis 3:4-5 Then the serpent said to the woman, "You will not surely die. For God knows that in the day you eat of it your eyes will be opened, and you will be like God, knowing good and evil."

We can choose the voice of God, "My sheep here my voice and follow me" or we can choose the voice of the devil and live in shame, guilt, depression, sin, fear and have a need for sympathy. Jesus said we will recognize His voice and a stranger's voice they will not follow. We have to choose to receive the love of God and believe we can be the love of God on the earth by simply believing God loves us. The reason Jesus came was to model the love His Father has for us so we have an example to believe in. Choose to be the love of Father God and Jesus to all and in doing so you will give glory to God and you will see heaven on earth in their faces. A precious walk with the Lord will be on your face too.

Fear and Love are Choices

Here are some fears most of us live in and may not even know it. Do you have insurance on your home and possessions? I know the law requires it in some cases but most of us would have it even if not required by law. Do you live worried about germs, food problems, running out of money? Are you living on prescriptions? Do you worry about who will get your junk when you die?

What did Jesus come to set us free from? Yes, Jesus set us free from the damnation of sin if we repent. But Jesus also set us free from the world if we live as He lived, believe as He believed and be baptized as He was baptized. We all came into the world naked but Jesus went out of the world naked. Jesus didn't even have clothes when He was crucified but Jesus left everyone of us the greatest inheritance ever. Jesus lived by faith and so should we. Our faith should be the inheritance we hand to our children! Not our junk. In Romans 14:23 we are told:

Romans 14:23 And he that doubteth is damned if he eat, because he eateth not of faith: for whatsoever is not of faith is sin.

As you can see *he that doubteth is damned* the only inheritance we should concern ourselves with is the passing on of our faith. We have some big decisions to make. Is your walk with Jesus passing on your faith or your doubts? Do you want to be perfect in your belief of God? Do you want to seek God with all your heart? Do you think the apostles could follow Jesus and watch a couple hours of television a night? The life of Jesus is a walking testimony of faith and is a demonstration of what having faith in God gives us power to do. Being in faith is living without worry, without fear, without depression, without sympathy and living in faith is knowing your needs are meet, faith is declaring the word boldly, *living in faith is worshiping God 24/7. Faith is knowing you are loved by God!*

I want to clarify denying yourself. Possessions are only a problem if you cannot give them up. Jesus slept in someone's house almost every night, so it must be okay with Jesus for us to have a home to live in. You know, our possessions are not a problem unless we worry about them to a point we live for them. A bad position would be anything that takes your mind of Jesus Christ. I live in a 1995 motor home. I thank God every day I have a nice clean quiet place to live in and anywhere Jesus sends me. I know in my heart I could give up my nice clean place to live, if Jesus asks me too. My faith in my Jesus makes my priority in life what Jesus needs done.

For me, faith makes my life simple. For example, after a couple days of not being able to eat properly, that is I could only eat small amounts of food, maybe a cracker at a time or my stomach would hurt. Then one night after not sleeping too well, I got up in the morning and went to the bathroom. My discharge seemed like water coming out of me. When I turned around to flush the toilet, I saw the discharge was blood. The toilet was full of blood. Immediately the voice of fear told me, 'Ron get to the hospital this is serious.' Again, immediately I turned my attention to God and as I flushed the toilet I simply said, "Jesus I am so glad you're with me." Then I went about my day as if nothing unusual happened. I haven't had a problem since and I have eaten as much as I want. Thank you Jesus your faith in me has made my life simple.

Look how faith made that situation simple. I didn't have to go to the hospital. I didn't have to wait in lines and have tests done. I didn't have to pray for a good report because *I already had one* and the Jesus plan comes without a co-pay. Thank you Jesus I love you too.

How or when do we know we are loved by Father God and Jesus?

I have heard of some people having some really cool experiences with God. Kind of like Saul being transformed into Paul. I personally haven't had a big day I can describe as *the day* except the day Jesus ask me to have Coffee Time With Jesus and

Jesus said we need to talk every day. Wow I guess that is my big day! Jesus and I have talked every day since and I would truly miss our talks if for some reason our talk didn't happen. Please don't put God in a box and expect Him to come to you in a certain way or on your terms. But please expect Him to come because you know in your heart He will come.

Yesterday I had conversations with three different people. All three are missionaries to foreign countries. The missionaries I am talking about have been to some really dangerous countries and in some really dangerous situations. They have stayed in these countries for extended periods of time. They know they are laying down their life to serve the Lord and that gives them great joy, a joy you can fill the room with as they tell stories of what happened there. Their trips have been very fruitful in numbers of healings and transformations. I dream about seeing miracles like those they have seen.

I have talked to pretty many missionaries in the past and have noticed a common thread in their conversations. They always talk about how the devil doesn't want them to go to wherever Jesus is calling them. So the devil always comes against them going with mischief that seems to escalade the closer they come to the departure date. Of course this mischief never stops them from going but it does make them more determined to go.

I wonder sometimes about how much we understand the love of our God. As you know I loved my wife and I knew Jenny loved me. Jenny knew I would lay down my life for her if someone threatened her well being in any way. Jenny knew that person would receive the wrath of Ron just for threatening her. I knew the same protection would come from my Jenny if someone threatened me. In fact, I used to say I feel sorry for anyone that threatened me in anyway because if Jenny heard about it the life of that person was in Jenny's hands until they apologized.

What I am trying to say is because of our love for each other we knew our protection for each other was automatic. I never prayed or fasted to have Jenny protect me and Jenny never prayed for my protection. We just knew we would lay down our lives for each other because of our love for each other. Jenny and I would have never known this type of protective love had we never spent time alone together. To know someone's heart we must spend time

118

with them and Jesus makes Himself available 24/7. Just as I knew Jenny would always be there for me I know Jesus will always be there for me because I spend quiet time with my Jesus. Is a lack of quiet time with Jesus holding you back from a precious walk with my Jesus?

I think the love of Our Father God and Jesus has for us is so much more protective then we can imagine. Knowing I am loved by Father God and Jesus truly brings peace into my life. I have their joy, protection and the loving forgiveness of them in my life. I believe we receive all this by having quiet time with them. Anyone who will ask them into their heart will receive their complete love. Please make time for my Jesus and you will never be sorry. Remember now is a good time to ask.

I have tried to explain this protection I walk in everyday to others. I tell people because I know I am loved by my Jesus and my Father God and I know their love is so real to me that I don't pray and fast for this protection. I just know by faith in my heart Their love and protection is real. I know for a fact if someone fired a gun at me my Jesus would take the bullet for me, this is not just a belief it is a fact. It was fact for David, Moses and the men of Hebrews 11.

Some people tell me the reason the devil never comes against me is because I am not a threat to the devil. I wondered if that is true. I believe anyone who knows or has experienced the love of Jesus in their heart is a threat to the devil. I believe the love of my Father God has for me has already been proven in John 3:16. The whole Holy Bible is a love story proving the Holy love my Father God and Jesus has for us all. All we have to do is believe He loves us and this should be simple for us to believe because they do love us and they have already proved their love for us. If you are listening, you too will hear them tell you they love you.

To me the protection of God is so complete I don't worry about details that most people worry about.

For example, I was walking in a campground the other day and saw a couple sitting by their campfire. The woman had a large book on her lap and there was just enough light of day for her to still read it. I walked up and ask if she was reading a Bible. She smiled and said no this is a book prevention magazine put out about foods we eat. She went on to say they do quote Scripture in this book so I believe it is biblical.

I ask her if she believes in God. She smiled and said they do. I ask if her and her husband prayed over their food asking God to bless their food, before they ate it. She said definitely. I ask her, do you believe Jesus does bless your food? Again she said yes definitely; then she realized where I was going with my questions and defended herself. She went on to say God gave us a brain and He wants us to use it. So I am using my God given brain and reading this health book to learn how to protect us from the things the government and scientist are doing to our food today.

I said I am so blessed. I simply believe God does bless my food so I am free to study and seek Him and grow with Him. I spend my time seeking the Kingdom of God and His righteousness knowing by faith God will bless my food to my body. My Faith is in my Jesus and Father God and so my faith has made my life simple. Thank you Jesus I trust you to protect me and I fully believe Jesus does protect me and Jesus even protects me from the food I am eating. Jesus said it and I believe it.

Mark 16:18 They shall take up serpents; and if they drink any deadly thing, it shall not hurt them; they shall lay hands on the sick, and they shall recover.

The lady with the food book and I continued talking about God until ten thirty or eleven o'clock that night and again for hours in the morning. My Jesus is so good to me and I see Him in everything and everywhere I go. Thank you Jesus! I love you too!

Food worries continued: *Organic apples.*

Here is a short story about organic apples. I believe this story shows how we can preach the Gospel by our actions.

I remember a young couple coming to my camper one morning to treat me to a bag of organic apples. The day before he came we had been together talking about the Lord. So they wanted to bless me with some of their organic apples they had grown on their organic farm. As he handed me the apples he was quick to point out 'these are organic apples'. I said, "That's okay I will still

120

eat them." The man was surprised by my answer and asked me, "Do you know what organic means?" He went on to tell me how special these apples are; as he explained to me what organic means. After he finished explaining to me, I replied, "That is okay. Like I said, I will still eat them."

My point is, we can have a simple life walking in faith with God or we can worry about everything we eat and how these foods will affect our health.

I hope you see my faith is in my God and what my God can do and I hope you see how by faith in my God my life becomes simple. I don't worry what the devil is doing. I don't worry if the devil perceives me as a threat or not and I don't worry if the devil is coming against me. I simply have all my faith in the protection of my loving best friend Jesus Christ. I keep my focus on Jesus and what He needs me to do today.

I see God as bigger than the devil, I have read some of God's Holy Bible and I believe God has defeated the devil. Worrying about what the devil is up to is putting your mind on him and that takes your mind of seeking my Lord. It is no different than seeking earthly junk. Seek the Lord with your whole heart, mind and soul! If I have to read and stay updated on all the things scientist are doing to my food so I can protect myself, I have just let the scientist replace my time with my Jesus with a fear of food.

I do not read health books like I used to. Yes, when we were young Jenny and I had a house full of the best foods and supplements money could buy. We read a lot of health books. When I realized my faith was in them instead of God I threw all our supplements away and all the books away and picked up the only book I'll ever put my faith in again – the Holy Bible. I do read other books about God but only to be inspired to know God more, for I believe our job here on Earth is to inspire people to come to know God more by our actions, our words, our life and for some us writing books like this one.

Is anyone perfect when Jesus calls them?

I believe my time here on earth is a gift from God and God simply wants us to choose to spend time with Him. People ask me "How do you find time to write?" I say, "Simple! I make time to write a priority. I know I am hearing from my Jesus while I am writing and hearing from Jesus is a blessing I can share in my writing." In my first 50 plus years of life I never had any desire to write. Reading and spelling are my worst subjects in school. Maybe a better question for me would be 'How do you write?' To me writing is a gift from my Jesus. Writing helps me stay focused on Jesus and the daily mission Jesus has for me. I love helping others come to a desire to walk with my Jesus. Writing is the way Jesus helps me share His love, so I love writing. Jesus encourages me daily and I love this new daily walk Jesus has me on. I must tell you my life wasn't always like this.

In my younger years I didn't have much discernment. I spent a lot of time holding unforgiveness toward others. Through discernment I have realized the devil helped me stay in my sin of unforgiveness. I listened to the devil a lot back then. Looking back I believe my real sin was not making God my priority. Oh I went to church and sang songs of how much I loved God with my hands held high; yes I checked that off my list every week, so I was good with God. I truly didn't think God was upset with me at all. The fact I lived the rest of the week in unforgiveness was normal for me and something I didn't need to deal with or if need be I thought I could deal with unforgiveness later on in life.

So how is Jesus transforming my life? Simply put, Jesus gives us all a desire to know Him. If you're like me you didn't listen to that desire. I was deceived by religion and I thought of religion as rules to keep me from having fun. Because of this misconception I really had no desire to know God any better than keeping the Sabbath holy by going to mass every Sunday. I mean I said the sinner's prayer so I was just fine. If God was talking to me back then, I had turned down my hearing volume to a minimum. Thank you Jesus for putting people in my path to bring me into a desire to know You. Ever so slowly and ever so gently, Jesus turned up the volume of my listening skills.

Jesus gently brought me to an awareness my actions of unforgiveness were hurting people and destroying my family. I even saw changes in my precious wife Jenny and in Jenny's love for me. I didn't like the changes that I saw in Jenny. To me, this was my wake up call. I knew I was not here on Earth to hurt people and I definitely didn't like the hurt I saw in Jenny's heart. It seemed

Jenny's love for me was fading. I realized a need to change something in my life, when all of sudden I became aware of three guys in my life.

Their names are *how, who* and *why*. These guys came into my life and they brought discouragement, despair and a feeling this is just a normal way of life. The devils – *how, who* and *why* that I was listening too even told me to go to church and you will see problems like mine everywhere. I started listening for the how, who and why questions people ask at church. I found they were everywhere. I listened to the questions people ask right as they came out of church like "How do you think they afford that?" or "Who does she think she is anyway?" or "Why does she wear her pants so tight?"

I knew something needed to change. I started listening to Christian talk radio, but found no help there. I listened to Christian music and for sure there's no help there. All I knew was I did not like who I was anymore. I knew I was supposed to love my neighbor as myself. I loved all my neighbors and they loved me. I was well thought of at the church. I volunteered to help everyone. But in my quiet time at home, I was actually a wreck. Jenny screamed at me one day. She said to everyone else you are so good but when your home you turn into a madman. Jenny was a fixer and I needed to be fixed.

Thank you Jesus, my Jenny went right to you. I had enough knowledge to know I could turn to God but I didn't know how. I thought God was in Heaven somewhere. I thought I was a sinner saved by grace and who wants to talk to or hang out with someone like that. Jenny begged me to turn to God. I believe it was her prayers that turned my thoughts to God. So I tried turning to God but He was foreign to me. I knew of God and I knew I needed to please God and I witnessed the relationship Jenny had with God but I didn't know how she came to know Him like she did.

As I started trying to turn to God, I noticed the first thing I was dwelling on or asking God for was how to make things right with my little Jenny. My thoughts were on Jenny and I didn't realize I was trying to operate in my own strength. I wasn't seeking God to know God. I just wanted God to help me restore my relationship with my precious wife Jenny.

As I tried to talk to God my past seemed to come into my mind all the time. When Vietnam thoughts came up and when I thought about the injustice in my life compared to others I started to realize I was still listening to the devil and not God. The devil was quick to show me all my faults and the faults of others, so I could hold unforgiveness towards them. The devil showed me why I didn't need to forgive and why it was okay to live like this. The devil even told me Jesus doesn't care. I didn't know to ask God for discernment. So I was just as mad and mixed up as I ever was.

One day, Jenny and I were in my woodworking shop and Jenny had just witness me lose my temper. Although she never felt threatened, Jenny hated seeing me so mad. She started talking to me about talking to Jesus. I told Jenny, "It's no use to me; I don't know how to talk to God."

In desperation, Jenny screamed at me. "Just talk to God like He is here in this shop!" I screamed back, "Why?" Jenny screamed right back at me, saying, "Because He is right here in this shop." I screamed back at Jenny, "God please talk to me like you talk to Jenny. Please help me Jesus." Then I looked at Jenny and screamed, "Are you happy now?" Jenny said, "YES" and Jenny went into the house. When I went into the house for lunch I smelled Jenny's homemade pizza in the oven. Wow! God was listening. I mean who told Jenny to make her home made pizza.

Jenny was right. When I was helping others, I was happy. Now Jesus wanted me to know why I wasn't happy being at home anymore. Jenny is the love of my life and she knew me at my worst and still loved me. I thank God when Jenny needed help, Jenny went right to God. Jenny told me to go to God and I was smart enough to listen, but I still really didn't know how. I didn't understand God. I thought working my tail off trying to please Him was all I needed to do and now I thought give me a break. It seemed God wanted more of my time. I wasn't sure how to talk to God and so far all Jenny heard me do was scream at God. But when I went into the house I saw Jenny had a joy and a peace that I couldn't understand.

I didn't understand how Jenny could be screaming at me one second and a second later go into the house and make her home made pizza for me. I mean, all I did was screaming at God for help. How on earth did that help? I didn't understand it then but to

Jenny I had asked God for help and she was standing in faith my Jesus help was on the way.

My walk didn't seem to change much but gradually I started turning all my thoughts to God and I started to have some quiet time to hear from God. I didn't know how to ask God for discernment but I started questioning my thoughts and questioning why I am even thinking about these things that make me mad. I had no idea God was working in me and wanted me to hear His voice. I had no idea God wanted me to dwell on Him. I really had no idea God wanted to be in my heart and God wants to be my best friend.

I guess a precious walk with my Jesus starts with us asking Him for help. I believe Jesus will put a Jenny in your life like He put into mine. That day I turned off the distractions and turned on my hearing and Jesus was right in my shop, waiting to talk to me. My motive that I didn't want Jenny mad at me anymore probably wasn't the purest reason for seeking God but God worked through my motive to improve my relationship with Him. And yes, God helped me learn the order of a relationship with Him. Jesus first and then all these things will be added; translated I needed to put Jesus first in my life and then my Jenny and my family would be okay.

One of the first things Jesus and I did together was to sit down and write a letter of apology to my family. Years earlier, I had written a letter of pure hate to my brothers, sisters and my parents. Now, Jesus was helping me tear down some fences I had created. Jesus and I became a team. I found the more I thought about Him the more I could love Jenny again and Jenny responded with her sweet love for me. Jesus removed my unforgiveness and replaced it with His love. Something else came into my life. Something I never expected... I started living in the forgiveness God has for me. I actually started liking myself. Thank you Jesus! I love you too!

In not too long a time I noticed those three guys – *who, why,* and *how* were gone also. Yes, I bid them farewell and told them to go back to? My new life had started, walking and talking to my Jesus was becoming the norm now and I was not mad like I used to be. Honestly, I felt alive again and in love with the cutest wife in the world. I had a long way to go and Jesus has been with me all the way. Jesus will never leave me or forsake me; thank you Jesus.

So to answer the question of *how do I find time to write?* I simply turned off the distractions and got turned on to the attraction of love Jesus has for me. From time to time this question still comes up "How do you find time to write?" and I answer their question by asking these people, "How do you find time to sin?" If I want to sin, I will make time to sin my priority. If I want earthly junk I will make getting junk my priority. Jesus said that where your heart is your treasure will be also. Sin is a distraction of the devil and the devil will use sin to break your belief in God. We have a simple choice to make daily – *Who are we going to listen too?* Jesus has replaced my desire to sin of holding unforgiveness towards others and myself with a desire to know Him. The coolest thing about listening to God is hearing how much God loves me.

So is anyone perfect when Jesus calls them? No one! Positively not! The apostles were far from perfect and Jesus transformed them daily. Jesus will transform you too! I know Jesus is transforming me daily and that is why I call it a walk. The best decision you will ever make is to answer His call. Don't worry about the starting point, just start! Remember, Jesus has all the answers. All we have to do is to start listening and start discerning. The best revelation you will ever receive is my Jesus is in love with you.

Priorities

Let us talk a little more about priorities. Is hearing from God your priority? Jesus said what we think about is what we become. Jesus said where your treasure is there your heart is also. So is your heart bent on sinning or on doing the work of God's kingdom? I think we will have a hard time doing the work of the kingdom if we are focused even a little on sinning. As we choose to walk with our Lord we will find sin will lose its grip on us and the Holy Spirit of truth will destroy the works of the devil when we give the Holy Spirit permission to dwell in us.

Want some more good news? The good news is when I sin I repent and I know for a fact I am forgiven and I simply thank God He loves me and we go about our day doing the work of His kingdom. Father God loves me and I know it! Pretty simple isn't it? I hope I don't sound too flipped about sin.

The thought of sinning is repulsive to me. If the same sin comes into my life to frequently I will stop what I am doing and make talking to Jesus my super first priority. I will turn up my hearing all the way and I will receive the good news from Jesus – I am forgiven. His forgiveness doesn't diminish the sin but it removes my guilt and allows me another new start. I love how you love me, Jesus.

While on my walk to the Lord, I have heard so many teaching on the devil and what the devil can do. I want to say I believe Jesus defeated the devil so by faith I have no need to war against the devil. The only time I spend casting out devils or the only conversation I have with the devil is to say, 'Devil, get out!' I refuse to focus on the devil and his evil. Instead, I do as Jesus commanded us. I focus on God and what He needs done. I know by faith God has defeated the devil so I know God will kick the devil out of my life when I focus on God no matter what the circumstances look like.

I will focus on Jesus, knowing Jesus is transforming me into the manifestation of His love. Sin is not love, it is evil. Jesus said what we think about is what we become. I want more than anything to become a son of God who serves God because I know I am loved. Jesus washed the feet of His apostles and in doing so Jesus was demonstrating the love of His Father through humility. I pray and hope to be a demonstrator of His humility. I pray and hope my walk is pleasing to my God in every way and I know by faith this is possible so I am going for it. I believe the love of Jesus is in me. I believe I can be His ambassador of love to everyone. Now I focus on forgiveness and hearing from my Jesus all the time. Look what God can do with my focus on Him.

Ephesians 1:17 That the God of our Lord Jesus Christ, the Father of glory, may give unto you the spirit of wisdom and revelation in the knowledge of him

With my focus on my Lord and bringing Glory to my Father of Glory I become the recipient of His Holy Spirit of wisdom and revelation in the knowledge of Him. Sure beats sinning and warring against devils all day.

Ephesians 1:18-19 The eyes of your understanding being enlightened; that ye may know what is the hope of his calling, and what the riches of the glory of his inheritance in the saints, And what is the exceeding greatness of his power to us-ward who believe, according to the working of his mighty power

Can you believe we have all this through belief? Faith comes from hearing the word of God. Well you just heard it! Do you believe it? I do!

Through my simple belief I live in the knowledge of knowing I am loved by my Father God and Jesus. This is so important to understand. Think about having 'The eyes of your understanding being enlightened.' We Christians need this so much more than an interesting sermon. I hear people talk about the end times are coming soon and yet at the Vineyard Church I went to last Sunday, they showed a skit form *Everybody loves Raymond* and then talked about other television shows, for about ten minutes from the pulpit. I seriously pray for that church.

We are to be enlightened 'that ye may know what is the hope of his calling.'

I believe the Hope of God is to call us into a belief. We are to be the riches of the glory of his inheritance in the saints now. Yes, you can live in the joy of God now. We can manifest His love now and in doing so we remove the fear of the end times, we will live without the need for self esteem, which is we will joyfully wash the feet of our fellow men. We will live without spiritual ties to earthly junk and be more joyful then those that have the earthly junk.

We will live in and according to *What is the exceeding greatness of his power to us-ward who believe.'* Please ask my Jesus to give you discernment toward understanding these Scriptures. The truth of God's Word is so powerful to transform our lives from hopelessness to eyes of understanding and to being enlightened to life everlasting. This is living without fear of death, without fear of end times and living to simply wash someone's feet today.

Belief is living and knowing 'what *is* the exceeding greatness of his power to us-ward who believes.' Yes, ask God to enlighten you into walking with the knowledge and wisdom to be His ambassador and believe He will because God actually wants you walk this earth in HIS love. Now that's my Jesus and He loves me.

Ephesians 1:20-21 which He worked in Christ when He raised Him from the dead and seated Him at His right hand in the heavenly places, far above all principality and power and might and dominion, and every name that is named, not only in this age but also in that which is to come.

To those who will believe Christ was placed far above all principality and power and might and dominion, and every name that is named, not only in this age but also in that which is to come. Here is another guarantee from God toward those who will believe. This same Christ lives in us.

The love of Father God protects me and I know it. Pretty simple, isn't it? The love of Father God forgives me and I know it. Pretty simple, isn't it? You know, God loves you when you wake up and see the toilet full of blood and say, "Thank you Jesus for being with me," and go about your day like nothing unusual happened.

Ephesians 1:22-23 And He put all things under His feet, and gave Him to be head over all things to the church, which is His body, the fullness of Him who fills all in all.

I believe these are baby steps toward the Lion and the Bear that David talked about and then look what we can do. Remember David stepped up on the fallen body of big old Goliath before David cut Goliath's head off. I believe David did so for my Jesus said in His word, "He put all *things* under His feet, and gave Him *to be* head over all *things* to the church." Yes. Why would I settle for impressing the people of this world when we can live with Jesus inside us?

My precious Jenny knew and had total faith when I was in my woodworking shop that morning. I screamed out for help from God, for God heard me and heavenly help from God was on the way. Jenny knew God would handle my sins. Jenny's forgiveness was homemade pizza and a smile of relief. God's forgiveness was Him showing me I had worth, because God loved me and cared for me. God's forgiveness allowed me to fall in love with me so I could be His love to others. Thank you Jesus I love you too.

Jesus opened my eyes to understanding and enlightened me that I may know the hope of His calling to become like Him. Jesus showed me the riches of the glory of His inheritance that I will spend eternity with Him for believing in Him now. Jesus went on to say we can see the exceeding greatness of His power manifest when we call on His name in faith like my precious Jenny did.

This is truly heaven on Earth. This is truth manifesting through our belief and we can walk in these gifts of truth everyday if we just believe Jesus and Father God love us and dwell in us and will flow their power through us. Now that's my Jesus and that is an exciting walk with my Jesus.

So what is your priority today? Could your priority be to come into a closer walk with our Lord and Savior? You know the priority we choose today will affect our future and our eternity. In our walk with our Lord we have all these blessings by faith. I hope faith is being taught in your denomination. I hope your church is teaching these Scriptures and not showing you reruns of *Everybody loves Raymond*.

We have all heard the term *backslidden*. Can you imagine believing in these Scriptures and then going back to your old ways? Neither can I! When we walk in the power of faith manifesting the love of God, we will never backslide. If your denomination is producing backsliders, you might want to question your denomination and ask Jesus how you can become a light in your denomination. Believe me, Jesus will show you how to be a light and bring His love into your denomination. We just read in Ephesians 1:18:

Ephesians 1:18 The eyes of your understanding being enlightened; that ye may know what is the hope of his calling, and what the riches of the glory of his inheritance in the saints

Believe it and become it to your denomination by simply asking Jesus for His words and His walk and being the loving understanding to all.

The forgiving love of Jesus Christ and Father God are so simple to me. The exceeding greatest of His power toward us who believe is overwhelming too me. The fact we can live in relationship with Jesus and our Father God 24/7 brings tears to my eyes. How can someone so great hang out in my woodworking shop and wait patiently until I call on Him for help? Oh my Jesus I give you my whole heart, I give you every drop of my blood, because every breath I take is a gift from you. My only request is to see as you see, love as you love and through your love bring Glory to my heavenly Father God and you Jesus. Yes, for your love toward me Lord I will willingly lay down my momentary life here on earth. Yes Lord, I want my fellow men to know Your exceeding greatness, by experiencing your love toward them.

People who knew me before Jesus entered into my heart will tell you they have a hard time remembering the old Ron. They ask me, "How did this transformation happen?" I tell them I started seeking God instead of earthly junk. A couple Sunday's ago, a father of four came up to me. After talking for ten minutes he said I would like to buy a camper and have my family and I follow you around for a couple years. I said, "In your quiet time, ask Jesus if that is His will for you. I believe we are to follow Jesus not the joy of another man, even if the man is in love with Jesus."

If you are really serious about walking with God in your heart, think about this: I have talked about the mercy of my Jesus and the goodness and loving forgiveness of God for these are so true. Do you know they come with a price tag for us? The price tag is we must be willing to give up our sinful nature. Christians tell me they have read the book and the end of the book says we win. They are right. But did you read how we win? Jesus tells us believers we are on a narrow path and we have to have a relationship with Jesus. I don't know any other way to know if our names our written in the Book of Life, except to hear this good news from Jesus Himself. Look what the alternative is, being cast into the lake of fire.

Revelation 20:15 And whosoever was not found written in the book of life was cast into the lake of fire.

I believe we are all called. But if we are always too busy to listen, we might not be chosen and Revelation 20:15 is pretty close to the end of the book. Believe and get your name in the book now.

Matthew 22:14 For many are called, but few are chosen.

Look what being too busy can do. We will miss what Jesus has for us to do today. We will miss our chance to be His love to someone and our business will steal our joy of the Lord and maybe keep us out of the book. Life is more than a sinner's prayer.

Matthew 25:44-46 Then shall they also answer him, saying, Lord, when saw we thee an hungred, or athirst, or a stranger, or naked, or sick, or in prison, and did not minister unto thee? Then shall he answer them, saying, Verily I say unto you, Inasmuch as ye did it not to one of the least of these, ye did it not to me. And these shall go away into everlasting punishment: but the righteous into life eternal.

Jesus never feared hearing His Father say 'Go away into everlasting punishment.' We can live without fear of hearing these words on our judgment day also. The life of Jesus is our example and I believe if Jesus was here on Earth right now He would not own a television or a computer even if these things brought 99% good knowledge in too His house. Yes 1% bad is too much bad for my Jesus and for my Jesus living in us. I am begging you to turn up your hearing, turn to the Lord and His wisdom, walk without distractions and hear Jesus call you by name. I have a joy, joy, joy down in my heart! I remember singing it and now thank you Jesus I know how you willed your joy to me.

Think about this for a moment. We have a source for wisdom. Our source is available 24/7. We need no batteries, no connections, no fees, and our source has died to show us He loves us and yet some of us turn to *Google*. Google has no love for us, its source is basically unknown, and Google will only know your name when you owe it money. You may have Google but I have a best friend and He wants to be your best friend.

Our walk includes our children not our television.

I remember a story I heard some years back. A fifth grade boy came home from school excited. He wanted his parents to sign a permission slip for him to watch a movie at school. The movie had a seen in it the parents deemed not appropriate for their son. He argued saying, "I will close my eyes during that part of the movie and it is only one seen in the whole movie, it is probably less than 1% of the movie, so it can't hurt me." The parents told their son, "We have a couple days before we have to decide, so let us to talk to God about the movie to see what God would think about it. Dad said we will give you an answer tomorrow son."

Their son came home from school the next day to find the house was filled with the aroma of brownies. The young boy got really excited as his mom took his favorite snack out of the oven. Mom put a homemade brownie on his plate and gave him a big glass of milk. She then told him before you eat, "I need to tell you; while I was mixing the dry ingredients for the brownies, I had to run to get the phone. Our cat jumped up on the counter and thought the dry ingredients were a litter box and did his business in the brownie mix. I tried to remove it all but I couldn't get it all but it was just a little so I don't think you will be able to taste the kitty poop in your brownies. After all, it was only about 1% of the ingredients, so don't worry it can't hurt you." Her son refused to eat the brownies and mom made her point about the movie. Thank you and praise you Jesus.

My point is I see people so worried about what they eat and how their food will affect their body. Yet the Lord in His word told us no deadly thing will hurt you and don't worry about what you eat.

Mark 16:16-18 Whoever believes and is baptized will be saved, but whoever does not believe will be condemned. And these signs will accompany those who believe: in my name they will cast out demons; they will speak in new tongues; they will pick up serpents with their hands; and if they drink any deadly poison, it will not hurt them; they will lay their hands on the sick, and they will recover."

I know Christians who will read and study health books for hours as if it can protect them. I hear Christians proclaim God is truth with their mouth and so they should for God is truth; I know God is truth. I wonder what non-Christians think of us Christians when we claim God is truth in Mark 16:18 as they watch us buying and studying health books to protect our own health. They hear us proclaim, "God gave us a brain so I must use it to protect myself." Where do those thoughts come from? In one word – *unbelief.*

Matthew 6:25 Therefore I tell you, do not be anxious about your life, what you will eat or what you will drink, nor about your body, what you will put on. Is not life more than food, and the body more than clothing?

Jesus tells us not to be anxious or worry about our food and clothes.

These Scriptures are promises of God toward us. Yet we seem to ignore these Scripture promises of protection, while at the same time we look at movies and filth on television and the internet as if it will not hurt us. Jesus tells us through Paul to cast down imaginations (television, internet etc). Do not watch movies and every high thing such as man's opinion that come against the knowledge of God. We need to bring these thoughts into a righteous discernment of the Word of God.

2 Corinthians 10:5 Casting down imaginations, and every high thing that exalteth itself against the knowledge of God, and bringing into captivity every thought to the obedience of Christ;

Our thoughts and our minds will be affected by what we see and hear. We must guard our minds by guarding the ports to our mind. I believe the news, the television and the internet are big sources of dung. I believe these sources can hurt us more then we might imagine. We are warned in 2 Corinthians to take every thought captive. I repeat *every thought*. Why? Because the best place to stop sin is in the first thought. It is easier to put out a match than a forest fire.

I believe our children shows are the worst. I have no way to prove that statement except to look at the results of watching it. The Messianic children I have met never watch or have very limited exposure to these sources of contamination and they have greater discernment, more respect for their parents, more peace and live much better productive lives. I realize there are a lot of variables in the statement I just made but please try to eliminate one variable at a time and watch your children grow into respectful, delightful, wonderful children of God. Now that is a wonderful walk with my Jesus. These things, television and internet are so easy to turn off. I promise you that in one month you will wonder how you find time to watch them.

I remember a saying I was taught as a child, 'Sticks and stones will break my bones but your words will never hurt me.' Now I know those words were straight from the devil. I had no discernment as a child but now I do and I have come to realize the importance of discernment. If we don't know who we are listening to, we are lost. To me, discernment is more important than any college degree.

Last year I attended a meeting where I was told about a mega-church that had a five million dollar budget just for the youth programs. They have around 2,800 children in this program. They have Christian dances with Christian music and Friday night at the Christian movies, Christian outreaches and Christian sponsored missionary trips. The administrators who set this up the program were alarmed to find out 98 % of their youth did not attend church after graduation for high school.

I see in the life of Jesus how Jesus allowed the children in His days to come to Him and He sat them on His lap and talked to them. We live in the days of Jesus now if we choose to. I don't see Jesus entertaining the children with loud music and movies. Jesus simply told the children stories. I am blessed to have experienced children in my hearing that stopped what they were doing and wanted to sit on my lap to hear the words Jesus gave me for them.

I believe the mega-church was giving the children Christian entertainment. Yes, the entertainment was Christian but maybe the message to our children was Christians need to be entertained and so when these children went off to college they sought entertainment and not God. Some of our churches do the same thing for their adults and we wonder why we have backsliders. We wonder why so many Christians think a little cat poop in their movies and television and internet etc will not hurt them but we see the results in our life. Maybe the reason God is not in our government, schools and public buildings; is we adult Christians are too busy being entertained.

One more thought on the importance of hearing and seeing. These same people who spend hours studying health books, will look at dung on television and the internet and think it will not hurt them. I am guilty. In my younger years I watched hours of television. I made television my priority for years and back then we only had three channels. Now thank you Jesus I have been set free from the television. Thank you Jesus I never got started on the internet.

I believe the devil has stepped up his attack with subliminal messaging. If you are watching television and or the internet, you need to be aware of what is going on. Like I said earlier, even 1% bad would be too much bad for my Jesus who had a super great relationship with His Father. So how do we think we can survive when most of what we are watching is totally bad and has subliminal messaging in it? If you think subliminal messaging isn't going on, well, I think you are making my point.

136

Matthew 16:6 Then Jesus said to them, "Take heed and beware of the leaven of the Pharisees and the Sadducees."

The leaven of today is our obsession with the need to be entertained. I call this leaven because we seem to have risen up a generation of people who have little regard for what the Holy Bible says. They will spend a huge amount of time leavening or raising up their earthly and fleshly dung. They do this at the expense of their own relationship with their spouse and children. Please, if any of this hits home, I want you to know it is never too late for a transforming relationship with my Jesus.

Please ask Jesus into your heart. Ask Jesus to help you make a brand new start, set some quiet time to let Him speak to you and allow Him to give you the words to transform your family and loved ones back to Him. Keep your focus on Him. Let Him set the priorities and let Jesus guide you every step of the way. All you need to do is deny yourself. Turn off the distractions.

Matthew 16:7-12 And they reasoned among themselves, saying, "It is because we have taken no bread." But Jesus, being aware of it, said to them, "O you of little faith, why do you reason among yourselves because you have brought no bread? Do you not yet understand, or remember the five loaves of the five thousand and how many baskets you took up? Nor the seven loaves of the four thousand and how many large baskets you took up? How is it you do not understand that I did not speak to you concerning bread?—but to beware of the leaven of the Pharisees and Sadducees." Then they understood that He did not tell them to beware of the leaven of bread, but of the doctrine of the Pharisees and Sadducees.

I tell you we have the same message today. A little doctrine in our lives will steal our joy, our peace and our love for one another. Contrast the momentary happiness of the little boy watching a seemingly harmless movie to the eternal joy of him seeing the priority his spiritual life is to mom and dad. Life is all about choices. Are we choosing distractions like television and internet or are we choosing to listen to the ONE who really loves you and making our God given children our priority?

Seek ye first the kingdom of heaven and our lives will line up with our precious God and our children will see the love and joy in your life and want what you have. They will be ready to spend time with you and they will want the relationship you have with the Lord. Yes all these things will be added. Jesus said it and we can live it if we choose too.

The Sinner's Prayer

Some Christians think they are saved by the sinner's prayer. People some times ask me how many people have you lead to say the sinner's prayer. I tell them none; but I have lead people into a relationship with God and into baptism of the Holy Spirit. I believe by faith my Jesus abides in me and I in Him. Listen to the words of Jesus as He speaks in John.

John 14:15-18 If you love Me, keep My commandments. And I will pray the Father, and He will give you another Helper, that He may abide with you forever—the Spirit of truth, whom the world cannot receive, because it neither sees Him nor knows Him; but you know Him, for He dwells with you and will be in you. I will not leave you orphans; I will come to you.

Because I know I am loved I keep the commandments, and I know Jesus prays for me personally, I have a helper, the Holy Spirit of God that helps me keep the commandments and the Holy Spirit abides with me forever. I have been adopted. Jesus chose me and I chose Jesus and Jesus came into me. Yes, I am born again, by water and Spirit. I am adopted by Father God. I keep the commandments. I have laid down my life willingly but it I do all these things without love I am useless. To me, a walk with my Jesus is more then reciting the sinner's prayer.

With this knowledge I no longer need the things of this world. I have Jesus abiding in me and my Father God abiding in me. This knowledge changes my everyday life.

Example: Last night I programmed my GPS for a Laundromat. The first one was 8 ten's of a mile from here. I went to the location and it was just a house not a Laundromat. I went to the second and no Laundromat. I checked the settings again and went to the third and no Laundromat. On the way to the fourth, I saw a Laundromat, so I quickly pulled in. There was a man standing in front of the laundry smoking a cigarette. He made a comment about the fact I use an old cooler for my laundry basket. I smiled and said it works for me.

As I was putting my clothes in the washer he walked over to me and asks, "Why are you smiling so much?" I told him, "Because I have my best friend with me." He looked at me and said, "Is that right? I didn't see anyone else in your car." I said, "My best friend is Jesus and Jesus lives inside of me and we talk every day." He looked at me as if to say, are you crazy. I said, "Jesus said in His word, my sheep hear my voice and I believe Jesus and so I hear His voice. He responded with, "Well I am a C. and E. man." I asked, "What's a C and E man?" He said, "I am a Christmas and Easter man."

To two of us talked about God until our clothes were washed, dried, and folded. In our conversation, he told me he was going to have breakfast with his 19 year old daughter from a previous marriage the next morning. He had not talked to her in nine years and was nervous about what to say to her. He reached out to her on face time or face net or something and she responded.

I told him I believe God loves for families to be restored.

I ask him if he knew, God gave you the desire to reach out to your daughter and God gave her the desire to respond favorably to you. I ask him to please rest and be in peace knowing if he asks God to help him in the morning with his words. God will give him the right words. God knows just what your daughter needs to hear and with your faith in God you will have the words she will need to hear.

As I said goodbye, he walked around the folding table and hugged me. He then said, "I am so glad Jesus put you in this Laundromat tonight." I said, "I am too." I said, "I need to show you something." I showed him my GPS and how I ended up in this laundry. He laughed and said, "I think Jesus wanted you to meet me tonight and I agreed."

Again, my life is so simple to me because I have my faith in my Jesus to give me the words in that very hour. And guess what? Jesus does! If I loved the things of this world and focused on what

Paul calls dung I wonder if I would miss this great Joy of the Lord. Listen to the words of John in 1 John 2:15-18 as He tells us what to focus on.

1 John 2:15-18 Do not love the world or the things in the world. If anyone loves the world, the love of the Father is not in him. For all that is in the world—the lust of the flesh, the lust of the eyes, and the pride of life—is not of the Father but is of the world. And the world is passing away, and the lust of it; but he who does the will of God abides forever. Little children, it is the last hour; and as you have heard that the Antichrist is coming, even now many antichrists have come, by which we know that it is the last hour.

I simply believe God has showed me. Our walk with Him is so much joy and knowing Him is exceedingly more joy for us believers here on earth today compared to the joy of believing or saying the sinner's prayer and I am saved. Can you imagine standing before Jesus for judgment and saying 'I am just a sinner saved by grace' and Jesus saying 'Yes, I know you believed that but all your life, but I prayed for you to come as a son of God in the glory of my love.'

On my judgment day, I pray I will not hear Jesus say, 'You passed me by as you drove over the speed limit to the soccer field and you forgot the elderly and the poor as you went to that expensive coffee house. Your made television and internet your priority over spending time with my children I gifted to you. You lived in the fast lane and you piled up dung really high but you were okay because you thought you were a sinner save by grace. You took pleasure in telling everyone I'm okay because Jesus sees my heart as you drove by the abortion clinic and never said a thing.'

I believe my life is changing and my priorities have changed. I have repented for my past and I am now moving on with my Jesus in my heart. Yes, that is right. I don't want Jesus to see my heart. I want Jesus to be my heart. I want Jesus priorities. I want Jesus compassion for my fellow men. I want to be the image Jesus died to give me. I want Jesus to tell me I am His favorite. That is my goal and Jesus said all things are possible and I believe Jesus.

Become an ambassador for my Jesus and introduce someone to the love of Jesus today and watch them run to Jesus to be saved. Believe me, Jesus will save them. It is His will that none should perish and the timing is now. Guess what else is of God? You, if you choose to be. Yes you can be the Joy of the Lord to someone everyday because Jesus will use your will and your timing to be His will and His timing right now. Isn't that simple?

In everything that grows out of the ground, trees, fruits, vegetables weeds etc., there are seeds that when planted will bring more of its kind. In the human sperm and a human egg is a child of God. Yes, big things start out small. I believe love is the same way. Start your walk today. Maybe all you have is a mustard seed of love in you but when given away the seed of love will grow and be free to be all it can be. We have the choice to hold on to it because it is all we have and in doing so we squeeze the life out of it or we can plant in faith that our God has more seeds of love to give us then we can imagine.

Let us prove to our Father God that we believe He sent His son to show us His love by becoming like the Son who is the Love of God. Sow some seeds of His love and watch Jesus transform these tiny seeds into a new you, a new city, a new America and a new world. All things are possible with God in us willing believers. It is never too late while you are here on Earth and Jesus is available 24/7 so right now is the time to offer Him your time.

Yes your time on Earth is your time. If you choose to give your time back to the giver; you will have peace beyond your understanding.

Decisions?

If you choose a precious walk with my Jesus; you must make a decision to walk with Him. The desire to walk with Jesus is an important part of the walk. The biggest and most important decision you will ever make during your life is whether or not to receive Our Lord and Savior Jesus Christ into our heart, which is to be willing to become one with him. They are waiting to be asked and they are ready and willing to come help us straighten out our lives. Please ask Jesus to reveal Himself to you and show Jesus you are serious by spending time reading His Holy Bible. Ask Jesus questions like He is setting right in the room with you, because He is.

The Holy Spirit is available to us 24/7 but we must believe He desires to be in us. I pray the Scriptures I gave you earlier are sinking into your heart. When you read His Word, ask Jesus to reveal to you the message He has in His Word for you. With God in us, nothing is impossible for us who believe. Listen to the truths of my Jesus.

Mark 9:23 Jesus said unto him, If thou canst believe, all things are possible to him that believeth.

Jesus has told us in His Word, "All things *are* possible to him that believeth." We have His word and I believe His Word because I know Him as truth, do you?

Don't be afraid to come to Jesus with your truth. If you have doubts, express those to Jesus and Jesus will honor your honesty. Listen to what the father of the child asks Jesus in Mark 9:24, 'Jesus helps my unbelief.'

Mark 9:24 And straightway the father of the child cried out, and said with tears, Lord, I believe; help thou mine unbelief.

If you are struggling with unbelief, please go right to your Teacher. The man in this Scripture struggled with unbelief and Jesus demonstrated the love of Our Father to him to help the man come into belief. Can you imagine struggling with unbelief and Jesus just pours His love all over you?

In most churches today if you came with unbelief like the man in Mark 9:24, our religious response to the man would sound like, 'If you want him delivered you need to get rid of the sin issues in your life, or have you checked for curses handed down, or you need to go see the deliverance pastor down the road, or I forgot to put on the full armor of God this morning so come back tomorrow or you need to ask the boy if he wants the devil dwelling in him?' Where is any of that in the Bible? Does any of that keep your focus on God and His righteousness?

For some reason, I cannot even think of responses like those coming from my Jesus? For me, those responses are *religion* and *Jesus is love*. No one can help you lose your unbelief faster and surer then the love of my Jesus. Jesus came to remove unbelief from us all and I believe Jesus rejoices when we turn to Him as our source of help.

Remember all things are possible to those that believe. Remember *all* the Gifts or fruits of the Holy Spirit are in you the moment you believe.

Galatians 5:22-23 But the fruit of the Spirit is love, joy, peace, longsuffering, gentleness, goodness, faith, meekness, temperance: against such there is no law.

Please ask God to help you follow Him and not religion of man. Jesus will help you live in the fruits of the Spirit 24/7. You will see these fruits start manifesting in you and you will see the people around you wonder what is different about you. There will be no arguing. Jesus never argued, no debating and no telling someone they need to change. Jesus never did any of that. Simply let the love of Jesus Christ flow through you and His love will transform your world around you.

Have you ever wondered why Jesus ended Galatians 5:23 with the words 'against such there is no law?' Have you ever heard of someone being locked up in prison for loving too much or being locked up for being too joyful, or being too peaceful, or for suffering to long or for being too gentle, etc? When we walk in these gifts of the Holy Spirit we will be transformed into the image and likeness of my precious Jesus Christ and when we are transformed we will need no law.

When we ask Jesus to come into our hearts and help us dwell on the life of Jesus, Jesus will come and Jesus will help us stay focused. Jesus told us what we think on we will become. So think on Jesus and become like Him and remember Jesus lived in all the fruits of the Spirit. By living in the fruits of the Spirit we too will fulfill the laws. The devil will flee and the Joy of the Lord is ours for free. It sure beats watching television or looking on the internet for something interesting.

Philippians 4:7 And the peace of God, which passeth all understanding, shall keep your hearts and minds through Christ Jesus.

Wow, Jesus says through Paul 'The peace of God will keep your heart and minds through Christ Jesus' if we believe. Paul says this is totally beyond all human understanding, so I don't understand it at all but I believe it all and I walk in peace.

Philippians 4:8-9 Finally, brethren, whatsoever things are true, whatsoever things are honest, whatsoever things are just, whatsoever things are pure, whatsoever things are lovely, whatsoever things are of good report; if there be any virtue, and if there be any praise, think on these things. Those things, which ye have both learned, and received, and heard, and seen in me, do: and the God of peace shall be with you.

If you truly choose to dwell on truth, honesty, justice, purity, loveliness, good report, thoughts of virtue, praise worthy, we are not just becoming like Jesus Christ but we are becoming His ambassador for these things and we will be on a precious walk

145

following Jesus Christ. If Christians would live this way there would be no need for law because the God of peace shall be in us all. Again, the Holy Spirit of God will bring the God of peace into your life, the Word of God says so and I believe, so I receive.

I choose to have the God of peace living in me. Having the God of peace living in me is the gift of loving others I can live eternally with. Live by Galatians 5:22-23 and Philippians 4:8 and we will have heaven on Earth. We will be living and demonstrating a life of no laws, no fear, no guilt, no condemnation and no shame. The truth is Jesus modeled this walk for us.

Please choose to turn off the distractions of the devil and let Jesus lovingly build a whole new you in His image and likeness. Jesus is talking, are we listening? The gifts of Jesus are available now to live in for eternity. Are you seeking the kingdom of God and His righteousness? Jesus made Himself available 24/7 so the time to dedicate your life to Jesus is now.

When we walk with Jesus, we walk in freedom from fear, freedom from the law and freedom from the bondage of sin and death. Oh how I love my Jesus freedoms. With gifts like these I will never need worldly junk again. We all will live eternally but I pray you have chosen to walk following Jesus Christ all the way into His loving judgment. I know Jesus is waiting for me; do you believe He is waiting for you. Do you believe your name is written in heaven?

With rewards like peace; why on earth would you not follow Jesus?

Deny Yourself

I wonder what most people today think of when they read Matthew 16:24:

Matthew 16:24 Then said Jesus unto his disciples, If any man will come after me, let him deny himself, and take up his cross, and follow me.

When Jesus told His disciples this, do you think it was a blank statement? Do you think Jesus said good luck with that guys and walked away? No! Jesus walked the walk and lived the life of loving forgiveness to all. Jesus did miracle upon miracle. Jesus taught His disciples and Jesus showed the disciples how to transform the world one heart at a time. I see Jesus as my source of knowledge, wisdom, power, life, hope and love. Jesus gave us everything we need to carry His message forward. Just as Jesus trained the apostles up in His ways, Jesus will train us up in His ways. Please read again the words of my Jesus:

Matthew 16:24 Then said Jesus unto his disciples, If any man will come after me, let him deny himself, and take up his cross, and follow me.

Jesus tells us to come follow Him. We follow Jesus by seeking Him with our whole heart. Let us deny ourselves by putting the needs of others ahead of our needs, or by making and tending to the needs of others a priority over our own needs. No one can have a precious walk with the Lord and not deny yourself. I know some people think to deny yourself means stop smoking, stop drinking, stop, stop, stop; rules, rules, rules and laws, laws, laws.

In a way these people are right. The difference is you don't stop drinking or smoking to get God to notice you or to notice your efforts so maybe God will love you. Actually the love of God is the complete opposite! God created you to be love and God already knows you. Those two facts in themselves will change your life if you believe or even give to your mind the possibility of believing them. These two facts will allow you to think maybe God could accept me. Think about the woman at the well. God accepted her in her sin and then she changed her lifestyle because His love for her transformed her heart.

You will deny yourself effortlessly when you know God loves you. The love of God is to enjoy yourself spending time with Jesus and Father God. They want you to delight yourself in knowing you are loved by God. Jesus didn't do anything to get His Father to love Him. Jesus did everything He did because He knew His Father loved Him. Jesus brought glory to His Father because Jesus knew His Father delighted Himself in His Son. We are simply delightful to Jesus and Father God when we seek him, deny ourselves, and take up his cross, and follow Him. Jesus is our best example of a loving life so follow His example and become delightful to God also.

Jesus told us He could do nothing of Himself.

John 8:28 Then said Jesus unto them, When ye have lifted up the Son of man, then shall ye know that I am he, and that I do nothing of myself; but as my Father hath taught me, I speak these things.

Here Jesus is telling us again the *Father hath taught Him and He speaks the words of His Father.* Jesus knew these things by faith. Speaking the words of His Father made Jesus delightful to His Father. Now we know Jesus will teach us, Jesus is our teacher and we will speak the words of Jesus by faith.

If you think giving up smoking or drinking or television is hard to do, then please simply give Jesus permission to transform your life and as He does you will gladly lay down these things and with joy you will thirst for my Jesus. This may sound stupid or far-fetched but I pray I will be killed standing up for my belief in how much Jesus loves me.

Yes Jesus was killed for saying the words his Father gave Him to say. I pray I too will be killed for my Father's words speaking through me and for my belief in my Jesus and I pray my walk here on this Earth will bring people to come into a desire to know God so intimately they too will lay down their life for an eternity with my Jesus and my Father God. Yes, for an eternity with Jesus and Father God I will gladly and joyfully lay down my earthly life. I actually pray for this boldness. I pray for the strength of Jesus to be in me so strong that I will pass the test. I will live my life to be persecuted for His glory. I desire to know God is so real I will prove their truth to everyone I meet.

When we realize we can do nothing of ourselves to bring glory to God, we will become teachable and allow God to teach us how to bring glory to God and they will show us their love for us. We will receive their love for us by faith and knowing we are loved will take away our desire to sin. I don't think Jesus had any desire to sin because He knew intimately how sin displeases His Father. For Jesus, the fear of the punishment for sin was nothing compared to the thought of being displeasing to His Father by sinning. A precious walk with my Jesus is a lot more than, "Hey, I am saved by grace."

I ask my Jesus to give me a revelation of understanding to help me realize I *do nothing of myself* but by choosing to have their Holy Spirit in me I will know He that sent me is with me. The Father hath not left me alone for I do always that thing that pleases Him. This is the power of the good news. He that sent me is with me, the Father will not leave us alone and we have the privilege to please Him. This is all we need, pray to know He is in you and with you. Please pray, 'Dear Jesus counts me in, I want my name written in heaven and I want more than life itself to please you.'

John 8:29 And he that sent me is with me: the Father hath not left me alone; for I do always those things that please him.

When you understand the love of God is in you, the love of God will teach you and the love of God will bring all things to your remembrance then and only then do all things become possible to you. You will pick up your own cross and you will lovingly forgive those that nail your feet and hands to it. This is the all things are possible my Jesus talks about.

I will follow my Jesus because I know my Jesus and my Father have shared their Holy Spirit with me to strengthen me, to teach me and to allow me the privilege to die for their Glory. I love you too, Jesus!

I want to point out some little changes in the language in Mathew and Luke. These changes are important.

Matthew 16:24 Then said Jesus unto his disciples, If any man will come after me, let him deny himself, and take up his cross, and follow me.

Luke 9:23 And he said to them all, If any man will come after me, let him deny himself, and take up his cross daily, and follow me.

In Matthew, Jesus was talking to the apostles while in Luke Jesus was talking to all of us believers. We are all supposed to deny ourselves. In Luke, Jesus said to pick up your cross daily. We are on a daily walk with Jesus and Jesus will give us whatever we need daily. Never worry about anything. My Jesus has already given us what we need. We have His heart, His mind and His eyes when we know we are loved.

Some years back, Jesus gave me an example of denying myself. Yes, I denied myself of fear by looking at the peace I saw in Jenny.

I remember camping in Kentucky in 2011 with a large group of about 80 Messianic families. That night, we were all gathered in a park building called the tennis center. The Park Rangers came to the tennis center to tell everyone in the campground to stay in the tennis center because a tornado was coming right in the campground. The rangers told us the tennis center building was tornado proof so we were all safe there.

This campground was loaded with trees and when trees fall on campers, the campers will be crushed. I chose to stay in my camper with my Jenny. So around 11:30P.M. I sat Jenny back in her wheel chair and proceeded to leave the tennis center building. Everyone tried to talk me into staying at the tennis center. I told them that I had prayed and God gave me peace about staying in our camper. I told them how I prayed and ask God to keep everyone's camper safe, so all the campers in the campground would be unharmed.

Jenny and I went to our camper, as I carried her in to the motor home the weather was eerily calm and quiet. Within seconds and at the precise time predicted the tornado came. Trees were snapping off all around my camper. The electricity went off and the wind sounded like a big train going through the campground. The rain seemed more like a wall of water hitting our camper. I turned on the headlights of the motor home and saw a tree down in front of my camper with a ball of roots probably 12 to 15 feet in diameter. Fear started to come into me but thank God I turned around and looked at my little Jenny sitting on the couch where I had sat her, Jenny's little face had zero fear and zero worry.

Jenny was sitting waiting for me to bath her and give her a snack like any other night. I looked at her little face and thought even in this stage of Pick's disease I am blessed to be looking at the example of peace in the storm Jesus gave me through Jenny. Yes, Jenny had the peace of Jesus and Jenny was modeling His peace for me. I had asked Jesus to keep us safe in the storm and Jesus gave me peace about being in the camper. But when the storm came, I needed a faith boost form Jesus and Jesus gave me one by looking at my little Jenny. All I needed was to focus on Jesus with faith in Jesus. When I saw Jenny's little face my faith rose up and fear left.

The motor home has a battery backup so even without electricity; I had 12 volt lighting. I bathed Jenny and gave her a snack like any other night. I ask Jesus for one more blessing before going to bed: I ask Jesus for sweet sleep. In the morning, I checked our motor home. We had absolutely no damage to our camper and we had slept like babies. Thank you Jesus for giving me peace! Thank you for removing my fear and for protecting your precious little Jenny and me.

In the morning, I started my generator and while I'm having my morning Coffee Time With Jesus I saw some men surveying the damage in the campground. They told me trees were down everywhere, the power was still off and these men were totally amazed to see not one camper was harmed. Everyone else stayed the night in the tennis center and was up most of the night praying for their own safety.

Here is another example of denying yourself. At most funerals, people cry because they have lost a loved one. They cry

151

because of their loss. A person who hasn't denied himself might cry because he is only thinking about himself. In reality, if we have denied ourselves like we are told in the Word and we believe in the truth of God's eternal life we should be rejoicing that our loved one went home to be with God. We should be rejoicing our loved one is enjoying their final reward.

Actually there are a lot of reasons a person might cry at a funeral but if we have lived the life Jesus modeled to us we will not grieve or have guilt about our loved ones dying. Study the Word to show yourself approved like the Word says and then you will be a good example of His love. Your loved ones will see you are light of His light and they will desire to have His light that flows from you so freely.

2 Timothy 2:15 Do your best to present yourself to God as one approved, a worker who has no need to be ashamed, rightly handling the word of truth.

This is the wisdom Jesus came to give us that is to rightly handle the Word of God. In doing so, we are gifted His Joy, His Peace, His Hope and His Love and His walk. When you ask God for these gifts and when you open your heart to receive His love for you, His wisdom and His personal relationship with you will give you peace of knowing your loved one will be rightfully judged by Jesus. Then what we call death becomes a celebration of new life with Jesus and Father God. Jesus destroyed death so believing in Jesus will turn funerals into a celebration of our new life.

We believers know Jesus conquered death. We should rejoice for there is no death. To believe there is no death takes faith and faith comes by hearing the Word of God and probably the first way to hear the Word of God is when we read His Word out loud to ourselves. We also hear the voice of God when we ask God into our heart to have a personal relationship with us. Jesus desires us to turn off the noise around us, the television, radio, internet, phones, etc.

All these distractions are devices that on occasion can be used to advance the kingdom of God and some use is good but it seems some of us are spending hours looking to other sources like

Google for wisdom instead of listening for the voice of God! You will hear the voice of God come directly into our heart. If these devices were a good source of wisdom from the Lord, the world should be giving their hearts to God and be transformed into His love by now. I ask you to please turn them off or at least limit your time on them.

The spirit of truth, is it for you?

I see people go directly to Google to get answers. I don't know who controls Google and I don't know the heart of the people who put their answers on it. Whoever controls Google controls your mind when you seek their answers. I know my source personally. I know my source loves me and my source has my very best interest in His heart. I know my source and we don't need a battery charger, smartphone, or the internet to talk to each other.

I choose to listen, to know and to have the spirit of truth in my heart. No walk with Jesus would be complete without knowing the spirit of truth lives in us. Our walk has to be and must be a living testimony of the spirit of truth or we will get derailed. Jesus is the spirit of truth and having Jesus dwell in me is having the spirit of truth in me.

If I am telling a story and add anything to the story I will get a twinge in my spirit. I pray to never add anything to His stories He has given me. For me to add anything to the stories Jesus has given me is like saying let me help you Jesus or did you forget this fact. Jesus is the spirit of truth and His stories are His stories.

Please read John 14:15-18 and see the spirit of truth and who can receive Him and who cannot.

John 14:15-18 If ye love me, keep my commandments. And I will pray the Father, and he shall give you another Comforter, that he may abide with you forever; Even the Spirit of truth; whom the world cannot receive, because it seeth him not, neither knoweth him: but ye know him; for he dwelleth with you, and shall be in you. I will not leave you comfortless: I will come to you.

The Spirit of truth dwells in me. I hear people say they are seeking truth. I believe they are seeking the knowledge of truth and not the Holy Spirit of Truth. They want the truth but they don't seem to understand truth is a Spirit of God dwelling in us. Jesus says the 'World cannot receive the Spirit because it seeth him not, neither knoweth him." How will they come to know God and His Spirit of truth unless we believers demonstrate it to them? How can we demonstrate the Spirit of truth? Jesus tells us in John 14:18 that He will not leave us comfortless: Jesus said *"I will come to you!"*

I love thinking of Jesus as my Comforter. I seek Jesus and His comfort comes. Jesus chose His words very precisely. We have the privilege of calling on Him who is the Spirit of truth 24/7. Jesus knew His walk would be over someday and He knew we would need more than a book to keep us on His narrow path. Our walk with our Lord is so important to God. They gave us their own Holy Spirit as a gift to teach us and perfect us into their perfect love.

As parents, we too should teach our children to hear the voice of God. In fact, we have an obligation to teach them who the Holy Spirit is and what His role in our life is. In doing so, we will have peace when our children start their own walk. We will know the Holy Spirit is in them and guiding them when they go to college or off to war. We will be at peace knowing no one can snatch them from our Father's hand.

The world may come against our children but we will know our loving God is in them and with them. We know they will be tempted by the tempter but our faith will be in the protection of our God and not in earthly knowledge. Tell your children to imagine having Jesus talking to them and telling them these special words of love because Jesus did tell us these words of love. That is the truth!

John 14:19-21 Yet a little while, and the world seeth me no more; but ye see me: because I live, ye shall live also. At that day ye shall know that I am in my Father, and ye in me, and I in you. He that hath my commandments, and keepeth them, he it is that loveth me: and he that loveth me shall be loved of my Father, and I will love him, and will manifest myself to him.

These are promises we can live with forever. This is a promise we can freely give our children. We will rest and live in faith that our loving God who gave us eyes to see our children as His children and He will keep His promise to them also. Jesus is with His Father and yet His spirit of truth is in us now if we believe. For if we believe we will prove our belief by living the two commandments not just keeping the commandments from fear of going to hell but by living them to show our love of God daily. Jesus said 'He that hath my commandments, and keepeth them he it is that loveth me: and he that loveth me shall be loved of my Father, and I will love him, and will manifest myself to him.'

I love my Jesus and my Father God and the best part is I know they love me. Living in the presents of God is where we live and have our being. Knowing Jesus will manifest Himself to us is peace. Our children should live in the peace of knowing Jesus is with them and in them and manifesting to them. Yes, the tempter will come but we will not fear for we have equipped our children with Jesus.

In John 14:16, Jesus referred to Himself as the Comforter. I fell prompted right now to make a distinction between comfort and sympathy. Comfort is feeding the hungry, clothing those in need. Jesus said, 'Give them your coat and hat as well etc.' Comfort is also praying for those in need. I believe the comfort Jesus is talking about is also His compassion. We give comfort through His compassion.

Sympathy is not comfort. The two do not mix. Jesus told me in my Coffee Time With Jesus the difference between sympathy and compassion.

I am making this distinction because as we walk with God we will need to comfort others through compassion not sympathy. The difference is sympathy allows you to stay in your problem. Sympathy always looks for more sympathy. Sympathy is always looking down in depression like 'Pray for me the doctor said the cancer is spreading, oh woe is me!'

Compare sympathy to compassion and you will see the compassion of Jesus is uplifting and compassion heals the problem. Compassion sees the need to help others and allows you to call on the name of Jesus to lift people out of a problem. Jesus showed us compassion to the people that nailed Him to the cross while being nailed to the cross by saying "Father, forgive them for they know not what they do" so we know compassion is forgiveness and forgiveness is love. I believe in true love of Jesus. Do you? Compassion is an overwhelming, healing love of Jesus Christ that we will experience and see manifest when we call on the name of Jesus in faith.

Luke 23:34 And Jesus said, "Father, forgive them, for they know not what they do." And they cast lots to divide his garments.

After all Jesus went through the last three days of his stay on Earth, He didn't look for sympathy. Jesus did the opposite. Jesus showed us the truth of His Spirit is compassion. He never trades His everlasting loving compassion for the devils momentary sympathy.

Please don't miss Jesus by being too busy to hear His voice or because you are looking for the sympathy of others. Just ask God to give you discernment in this matter and He will. If you think you are walking in a need for sympathy, please turn off the distractions and start talking to God like He is right in your living room because he is! I don't think we even need to ask God for His comfort because in John 14:18 Jesus tells us, "I will not leave you comfortless," and Jesus promises us, "I will come to you." Remember Jesus is the Spirit of Truth. Therefore, you can count on His comfort no matter what the circumstances look like.

I believe we miss the Joy of our Lord and the comfort of our Lord and the peace of our Lord when we are too headstrong operating in our own strength to hear His voice. Please turn of the distractions of this world and turn on the attraction of life eternal with my Jesus. Listen again to His words here in John 14:18 an John 15:9-13.

John 14:18 I will not leave you comfortless: I will come to you.

John 15:9-13 As the Father hath loved me, so have I loved you: continue ye in my love. If ye keep my commandments, ye shall abide in my love; even as I have kept my Father's commandments, and abide in

156

his love. These things have I spoken unto you, that my joy might remain in you, and that your joy might be full. This is my commandment, That ye love one another, as I have loved you. Greater love hath no man than this, that a man lay down his life for his friends.

Please people read these verses over and over until your desire to be distracted by television and the rest of the world leaves you because I know for a fact the love of God will come to you and comfort you the same way Father God comforted Jesus. Television comforts by distracting us from reality. Jesus comforts us by bring us into His reality of hope, peace and forgiveness.

Last Sunday December 6, 2015, I went to the Vineyard Church on Round Top Road in Cincinnati Ohio. The assistant pastor gave us a message on solving conflict. He started with showing a funny clip from the show *Everybody loves Raymond* about conflicts. He then named two other shows on television he thought were cool. He even asks for a show of hands to see how many people agreed with him. His reference on his PowerPoint presentation was from a book that he had read. I think there were a couple hundred people in attendance.

During the service, I cried softly. My spirit cried and I thanked God for His Word that says our prayers will be answered. My friends who asked me to come were excited to introduce me to some of their friends after the service. As these men and I talked, I saw Julie get a little upset as she talked to her mother on the phone. Her mother could not come to service because her liver was acting up during the night.

Julie handed the phone to one of the men standing there and asks him to pray for her mom. He immediately commanded the devil to take their hands of her liver and come out of her and he commanded the pain to leave, in the mighty name of Jesus. He then asked, "From the scale of 1 to 10, how's your pain?" Mom said it was still the same. He prayed again and asked the same question again. Mom said that she was still in pain. He told her the church was having their prayer rooms open at 7 P.M. and asks her to come tonight and receive more prayer. He then handed the phone to his friend to have him pray.

I am not sure why but his friend handed the phone to me and ask me to pray. I had already been asking God what He wanted to say to this woman. So I asked her if she knew God loved her. She said, "Yes, I know God loves me." I replied, "Great! Because if you know you are loved by God and you know that for sure then sometimes we don't need to pray for healing." I then talked about Paul being bitten by the viper as he put more sticks on the fire after the shipwreck. Paul never prayed. He shook the snake into the fire and then went on eating. I said, "Sometimes, a prayer of faith is no prayer at all. The word says 'the prayer of faith will heal the sick and not the prayer of fear.' Paul didn't pray he just continued to eat."

I told this woman when I read this I closed my Bible and asked God for that kind of faith. I told God when a snake bites me I don't want to come running to you in fear but rather I want enough faith to continue with the work at hand. I went on to tell this woman how a couple months ago I had a stomach problem for three days. I could barely eat or drink. The third day I went to the bathroom and realized my discharge was all blood. Upon seeing the blood, I immediately heard a voice say, "Ron get to the hospital, this is serious." But as I flushed the toilet, I heard in my heart, "Thank you Jesus for being with me." And I went about my day as if nothing had happened.

Julie's mom said she had three dreams during the night. In all three dreams she thought she had filled the toilet with blood and told her husband to call 911. She said isn't it amazing how God put us together on the phone today and how God prompted you to tell your story. Julie's mom said, "I am just going to thank God He is with me all day." Now that's my Jesus and His plan is so simple.

As we Christians walk our walk, some of us want comfort, we want to be entertained, we want happiness, we want fulfillment, we want people to listen to us and show respect, and most of all we want someone to love us. The answer to these wants is our living God in us.

A relationship with God is comfort. It is entertaining, it is Joyfulness and people will want to hear you speak, and the love of Jesus will come into us and we will overflow on to everyone we meet, His love, His joy, His comfort, and His light. These are the gifts of having a relationship with God. Please don't miss them by being distracted with things we can so easily turn off or even stomach pains that seem so real.

You will not find the gifts of our God on a cellphone, television, internet, an education degree or even by loving a pet. God's gift of comfort is not a lazy boy chair in your living room and a big screen television and your dog sitting alongside of you. The gifts from God transcend all our worldly distractions. Godly comfort is His protection in us. Knowing we are protected, knowing God will give us the words and the actions to lead others to His love. Godly comfort is knowing we walk with the Holy Spirit in us, guiding us, cleansing us and forever loving us. There really is no earthly comfort to compare the comfort of our Lord. Wow, I think I just gave you a new definition to the phrase *keeping up with the Jones*. Maybe the phrase should be *keeping up with the Joy of the Lord!*

Here on Earth we usually set goals for ourselves. We are taught by the world to climb a ladder to success. Some even call it clawing your way to the top. Contrast that with a Godly walk with our Lord. On a Godly, walk we start by talking to the CEO, we have personal relationship with the president; we live in the blessings of the top official. We have favor and comfort and communication with the one who never deceives us, the one who never leaves us, the one who only looks to our best interest and the one who has a promise of eternal life. The best part is while on our journey to the top we share the Good News with everyone and help them instead of trying to outperform them. All this is possible by believing we can live in the fruits of the spirit. Try to find that on any company mission statement.

Yes we start our walk by talking to the one who is the Truth, who is the Creator, who is the Comforter and the One who actually loves us. I want to be defined by the love of God flowing through me because I believe that is how I bring Glory to my Jesus. Jesus brought Glory to His Father by simply being the love of His Father to everyone He met and so can we. I believe God loves me, do you believe He loves you?

Here is a story about Ray, a man who searched for truth. He was a Baptist minister for years who was searching for truth and believes he found it in the Catholic Church. Ray left the Baptist church to become a priest in the Catholic Church. I listened to his whole CD. So much of what he said was true and I believe I learned a lot. Although there seemed be something about the CD that upset my spirit. After listening to it I became upset. I went for a walk and could not quiet my spirit. I came back to my camper and asked my Jesus what I heard on this CD that makes me this upset. The whole CD was short stories about Ray leading people into his truth.

I sat quietly in my camper. Although something inside me wanted to scream, very slowly, Jesus started to bring my focus to certain parts of the CD. I realized every conversation Ray had while being a Baptist minister concerned bring people into his belief the Baptist was the one true church. As Ray grew in truth, he came to the conclusion the Catholic Church is the one true church and now he is armed with the true truth and wants to bring everyone into his truth again.

Ray is extremely well-versed and makes his points about the Catholic Church very well. On that CD, he tells a story about being invited to a friend's house for dinner. His friend invited another couple who just happened to be Catholic priest who in his search for the truth, believes he found it and left the Catholic Church to be a Baptist minister. Ray mentioned that the couple who invited them where expecting a fireworks and Ray and the other man didn't disappoint their friends. Ray argued point for point and won.

In part of the CD, Ray talks about arguing with his son-in-law who is a Baptist minister about his beliefs. Ray chuckles and very proudly states that His son-in-law admitted to his wife that Ray is right. The son-in-law said although I believe Ray is right, I will not become a Catholic because to do so would be admitting Ray is right and I am wrong. As my mind was going over these stories on the CD, the Holy Spirit brought me a question. The Holy Spirit asked me, "Ron, in your writings; what is the one thing you tell people God never does?" I thought for moment and realized the answer is God never argues. Truth is truth and truth doesn't argue for that would mean God is arguing with Himself.

Arguing sets up a confrontation where someone has to be right and someone else has to admit that he is wrong. I have yet to see an argument transforms a heart. Jesus never argued. Ray actually confirms this point with the son-in-law story. I think how

160

sad, I mean the love of Jesus is reduced to who is right and who is wrong. Isn't that how most wars start? Jesus clearly showed us how to build the kingdom of God through the fruits of the Spirit and arguing is not a fruit.

I do believe Jesus liked fireworks. I believe Jesus set some fireworks off everywhere He went. Jesus never argued. Instead He just proved that he is the truth manifesting in front of you. Yes, truth is manifested through truth God is manifested by God and we don't have to argue about God for we just let God prove His word is truth.

In this story you will see what I call *Jesus fireworks.*

Mark 3:1-5 And He entered the synagogue again, and a man was there who had a withered hand. So they watched Him closely, whether He would heal him on the Sabbath, so that they might accuse Him. And He said to the man who had the withered hand, "Step forward." Then He said to them, "Is it lawful on the Sabbath to do good or to do evil, to save life or to kill?" But they kept silent. And when He had looked around at them with anger, being grieved by the hardness of their hearts, He said to the man, "Stretch out your hand." And he stretched it out, and his hand was restored as whole as the other.

I love my Jesus fireworks and the grand finally is yet to come. Don't worry if you don't believe me. I won't argue with you because I know my Jesus will gently convict me if I am wrong. I thank God He has made me smart enough to repent like the word says and I will be set free to be His love to everyone I meet. Stretch out your hand and I will pray and I will watch my Jesus heal you. Jesus never argues but Jesus does prove beyond any doubt He is who He said He is. I am being transformed daily and I pray you are too.

How do we take up our cross and follow Jesus?

I guess we need to define what a cross is. Some people think sickness is a cross, so they are okay with being sick? Some people think our cross is doing without, so being deprived is their cross? Some people think sorrow is their cross, so losing a loved one is their cross? If you claim a burden to be your cross, does that qualify your burden to be your cross?

If the cross is sickness, why did Jesus heal the sick? If the cross is being deprived of something why did Jesus say you will not lack anything? If sorrow is the cross, why did Jesus tell us to rejoice in our trials? If we claim a burden as our own, does that mean by choosing the burden we get to choose what cross to carry? If so why did Jesus say 'Father if it be your will take this cross from Me but not my will but thine be done?'

Luke 22:42 Saying, Father, if thou be willing, remove this cup from me: nevertheless not my will, but thine, be done.

I believe the cross or cup as Jesus calls it here is our choice. We either believe in Jesus and the relationship we have with Him or we believe the devil that says there is still death, sorrow, depression, self pity, and unforgiveness. And if we listen to the devil he will gladly give you fear, take away your hope, your health, isolate you, and keep you in captivity. Yes, we have a choice to believe God and the fact His kingdom is at hand to help us overcome the trials at hand. Or we can choose to believe the devil and his momentary feelings of happiness through drugs, alcohol, and self indulgences.

For me, the cross is unbelief, the sin of the world is unbelief, and the trials that come to try your faith are simply to test our belief. Every decision we make in life speaks to others of our faith or our unbelief. If you are walking in fear or any of the trials I mentioned above then you are listening to a devil. If you don't believe me, please check your Bible. The Word of God says God has life not death, God has joy not sorrow, God has compassion not depression, God has forgiveness not unforgiveness, God has living for others not selfish self pity, God has freedom from the sin of unbelief by promising the removal of sin as far as the east is from the west. I believe and I know for a fact our daily cross is struggling with unbelief.

God our Father wants to strengthen us so we never waiver. We need to praise God for our trial even while in our trial. I mean, trials prove our belief. How could we possibly know how strong the faith of Jesus was until we saw how big the trial of Jesus was? Father God loves us so much if need be He will send an angel to strengthen us. If you don't believe that, please read your Bible for the word of God says Father God sent an angle to strengthen Jesus.

Luke 22:42-44 Saying, Father, if thou be willing, remove this cup from me: nevertheless not my will, but thine, be done. And there appeared an angel unto him from heaven, strengthening him. And being in an agony he prayed more earnestly: and his sweat was as it were great drops of blood falling down to the ground.

Personally I cry when I read these Scriptures. I dwell on the strength of Jesus to trust His Father and I ask my Father to strengthen me with the strength He gave His son Jesus. You know, I want my test. I want my life here on Earth to bring glory to my best friends Jesus and Father God. I want my Father to know I will trust that He loves me no matter what the circumstances look like and I know my Jesus will send an angel to strengthen me if I start to falter.

I thank my Jesus for telling me in His word that I will have an angel to help me in my trial. Jesus comforts me, Jesus sees me as His 'little one' and I know I am protected in my trials. I believe because I have seen the truth is the Word of God. I believe by being born again of water and the Holy Spirit, I am His child!

Matthew 18:10 See that you do not despise one of these little ones. For I tell you that in heaven their angels always see the face of my Father who is in heaven.

Mark 9:42 Whoever causes one of these little ones who believe in me to sin, it would be better for him if a great millstone were hung around his neck and he were thrown into the sea.

I love being one of my Father God's 'little ones.' I love knowing I am protected. I love knowing my strength is in my Father God and Jesus who dwells in me through their Holy Spirit who lives in me. I love knowing my angel sees the face of my Father who is in heaven right now. I believe when my angel is looking into my Father's eyes they see His joy and I want more than life itself to see My Fathers eyes light up with joy when He sees me.

John 16:7 Nevertheless I tell you the truth; It is expedient for you that I go away: for if I go not away, the Comforter will not come unto you; but if I depart, I will send him unto you.

I love walking in the promises of God for I know God has sent His Holy Spirit to me. Now that is a promise from God that I can live with, I can live in and I will never doubt His presents in me.

Why should we praise God in a trial?

1 Peter 1:6-9 In this you rejoice, though now for a little while, if necessary, you have been grieved by various trials, so that the tested genuineness of your faith—more precious than gold that perishes though it is tested by fire—may be found to result in praise and glory and honor at the revelation of Jesus Christ. Though you have not seen him, you love him. Though you do not now see him, you believe in him and rejoice with joy that is inexpressible and filled with glory, obtaining the outcome of your faith, the salvation of your souls.

I pray for my trials. I want the genuineness of my faith proved beyond any doubt. Some Christians tell God how much they love Him all day long. But sadly, it seems by witnessing their walk they go out into the world and seem to prove to everyone they don't understand His love at all. If your trials come and your response is 'Why did this happen to me?' or 'Don't you love me, God?', I believe you are proving to everyone that you have no faith or knowledge of how much God actually love's you, or your belief is very shallow and driven by circumstances.

Do you realize these responses come from our heart? For Jesus said out of the heart a man speaks his beliefs. I believe we live what our heart believes. A precious walk with the Lord will have trials and we will praise God in the trials. If we believers simply believe that we are His little ones and therefore we know it is not our strength but it is our belief in God that will allow us to smile in our trial.

The simple truth is God loves us and doesn't want even one of us to perish. Jesus said trials will come but woe to the person who brings them. We need to believe we are adopted in this relationship with Him by our willingness to be baptized by the Holy Spirit. We receive a complete package when we receive the Holy Spirit into our heart; nothing is held back. Jesus never holds any of His love back so we can trust, believe and have all our faith in Him.

We prove our faith in God by praising Him in our trial, knowing we have the same Holy Spirit that raised Jesus from the dead in us. Believing in God means we never die so why do we believers cry at the transformation of a loved one? Do we really believe or is crying at a funeral really telling everyone we need to spend more time in the word. Please read these Scriptures again.

Luke 22:43-44 And there appeared an angel unto him from heaven, strengthening him. *And being in an agony he prayed more earnestly: and his sweat was as it were great drops of blood falling down to the ground.*

Here Jesus is showing how to carry our cross. We carry the cross with the help from Him. We need to know we are never alone. We see here Jesus was in agony not self-pity. We see here Jesus in His agony prayed more earnestly and not, "Oh God! Where are you?" When my cross comes I pray I have been strengthened by my Jesus to not only carry the cross but to be a light of the Fathers love so others are strengthened. I believe the prayer of Jesus was Father let the carrying of this cross bring Glory to You.

Look at what the Word of God says about trials and picking up your cross.

Romans 8:18 For I reckon that the sufferings of this present time are not worthy to be compared with the glory which shall be revealed in us.

Matthew 5:11-12 Blessed are ye, when men shall revile you, and persecute you, and shall say all manner of evil against you falsely, for my sake. Rejoice, and be exceeding glad: for great is your reward in heaven: for so persecuted they the prophets which were before you.

Persecution is a choice we must willingly take on. I call it a choice because we can deny our belief in Jesus and live another day. We read in the Word. The apostles deny Jesus before they were baptized in the Holy Spirit. Persecution comes in many different forms and we know from whom it comes from. Sickness is not persecution, lack is not persecution. True persecution is standing up for your beliefs in Jesus Christ. Again Jesus is our example and Jesus stood up for His belief in His Father's love for Him.

1 Peter 1:7 That the trial of your faith, being much more precious than of gold that perisheth, though it be tried with fire, might be found unto praise and honour and glory at the appearing of Jesus Christ:

Yes, I pray when my trial comes I can stand strong in faith singing praises to my God for letting me be tried. I believe the only way to have the strength to be tried as Jesus was tried is for us to understand we are loved by God. The trial Jesus went through brought glory to Father God by Jesus simply believing Father God loved Jesus and the trial was for a greater good. We too can bring glory to God by believing in the love Father God has for us and by being steadfast in our belief that the trial we are in is going to bring glory to God. Jesus the man brought glory to God and so can we.

James 1:2-4 My brethren, count it all joy when you fall into various trials, knowing that the testing of your faith produces patience. But let patience have its perfect work, that you may be perfect and complete, lacking nothing.

James tells us to count our trial as all joy. I knew Jenny loved me so I knew I would suffer anything to bring joy to her. Now I know Jesus loves me and I will do anything to bring joy to Him.

Read what the apostles went through and how it did not slow them down at all; in fact it brought joy to them.

Acts 5:40-42 And they agreed with him, and when they had called for the apostles and beaten them, they commanded that they should not speak in the name of Jesus, and let them go. So they departed from the presence of the council, rejoicing that they were counted worthy to suffer shame for His name. And daily in the temple, and in every house, they did not cease teaching and preaching Jesus as the Christ.

I want my trial, I want to bring glory to God and I hope you do to.

Is The Law Fulfilled?

This seems to be an age old question. Here is a short story that I hope will clarify your belief in the law. I pray you will take the question 'Is the law fulfilled?' to God and listen for His words.

When I ask this question I sat quietly and started thinking about the day I proposed to my Jenny. The day I ask Jenny to marry me she said yes. Praise God and praise Him some more, thank you Jesus.

Then Jenny said I have two rules for you Ron.

First rule: Jenny said, "No one hits me. If you ever hit me, don't fall asleep in my presence because I will get the biggest frying pan I can and I will smash you head." Then Jenny said again, "No one hits me." I told Jenny that she could cross that one off the list because I will never hit her. I had a bad temper back then and I believe Jenny was justified in her concerns. Jenny had come from a background of being in foster homes all her young life. Jenny never liked to talk about her youth but I could tell she had been hurt and now she was just wanted me to understand the ground rules for our marriage.

Second rule: Jenny told me if I ever cheated on her she could not live with someone she could not trust and our marriage would be over. Again I told her to cross that off her list because I will never cheat on you Jenny.

I am proud to say I never hit my Jenny and I never cheated on her. Jenny gave me the law and I up held her laws by never breaking them. My point is this: the fear of being murdered with a frying pan and the fear of having Jenny leave me was not my motive for never breaking her laws. The fear of those consequences did not even enter my mind. You see, I know Jenny loved me and I loved her and I knew in my heart I would never ever do anything that would break her heart and her belief in me.

Actually, I knew in my heart that if I had ever lost my temper and hit my Jenny I would have killed myself to protect Jenny from me and to protect my Jenny from feeling the need to commit murder to protect herself. If I had ever broken her trust in me, I believe my heart would have exploded just looking at the hurt of distrust in my Jenny's eyes. I believe it would be easier for me to die than to see the hurt in my Jenny's eyes. There is no momentary happiness on this Earth that could replace the everlasting love Jesus gave Jenny and me to share.

I am positive Jesus is the same was way. Jesus gave us His laws and Jesus let us know the consequences for breaking His laws. Bible history proves the fear of the consequences or going to hell was not really a good motivator to keep us on the narrow path to God. For most people, the artificial, momentary happiness of sin out weighted the fear of going to hell.

I believe Father God and Jesus decided to make a new covenant with us. This new covenant would be built on us knowing for a fact the devil is defeated. In the new covenant, fear was replaced with trust in God, death was replaced with eternal life in God and momentary happiness was replaced with eternal joy of the Lord, weakness was replaced with strength in God, hate was replaced with the love of God. Unforgiveness was replaced with God's forgiveness, the sin of the world or unbelief has been replaced with belief in God.

I believe the greatest gift from God is communication with God and God restored our communication with Him and Jesus became our Teacher. Keeping the laws of God became a precious walk with our Lord. This new Covenant with our Lord and Savior Jesus Christ is ours now through belief and faith in what Jesus accomplished by coming. The gifts of forgiveness and grace are ours by receiving the Holy Spirit while being baptized with water and the Holy Spirit of Jesus and Father God today. How could we possibly fall in love with someone we never talked too or heard from or had intimate conversation with?

Please take time to read your Holy Bible and you will know Jesus came to show us the love of our Father. Jesus was also showing us by example why He could not sin. Jesus knew He was loved by His Father. Therefore he didn't what to break the trust in the love they had for each other. I believe Jesus knew if He had sinned He would not be able to look His Father in the eye ever again.

Jesus knew the hurt in His Father's eyes and the pain in His Father's heart would be too much for Jesus to bear. Jesus probably told His Father to cross sin off the list because Jesus knew He wasn't going to sin. Jesus probably told His Father to cross unforgiveness off the list because He will live in His loving forgiveness, no matter what the trial. Jesus walked here on Earth without these worries because Jesus was baptized into the Holy Spirit which gave Him the strength to keep his heart his mind and his eyes fixed on His Father's love for Him.

I believe the joy of knowing I have the love of God in me is my joy and my strength and my motive for keeping my eyes fixed on my Jesus and His kingdom work. By keeping my mind fixed on my Jesus and knowing He gave me the gifts of the Holy Spirit, I will be the love of Jesus to everyone I meet and remember Jesus said against such there is no law.

The love of Father God and Jesus is so complete for us that my Father had to turn His eyes away from His only Son at that time so Jesus could become sin. I believe Jesus became the sin of the world to break the cycle of sin and Jesus broke the cycle of curses that existed back then. I believe Jesus became all the sin of the world to prove to us by example that even if we sin every sin of the world, we too could be forgiven just like Our Father forgave His first Son. Yes people repentance is a gift from God to His sons. Every Christian knows our Father forgave His son Jesus and by the example Jesus gave us. We should walk in the revelation of knowing we live in His forgiveness today. Please be baptized into the adoption of your true loving Father and His son, my Jesus.

We all know Jesus became sin and was forgiven. Now because of the loving forgiveness of our Father we believers know Jesus is walking in Glory with our Father. Jesus told us in the Scriptures we too can walk in His Glory every day. We too can have the purity of His heart in our heart and the purity of His heart will shine through our eyes everyday to help people recognize His love in us.

Please make His loving forgiveness personal to you. Please receive His loving forgiveness, receive by studying his Scriptures on forgiveness. How will you receive if you don't know His forgiveness exists? And how will you know it exists unless you have been told in the Word? Please let His forgiveness fill your heart. In doing so, you will fall in love with who Jesus created you to be. We are all created to walk in His image and likeness which is His loving forgiveness to all. If you struggle with forgiveness toward someone, simply go to the ultimate forgiver and ask Jesus for help. You will be glad you did. Pure freedom to become His love will be your reward and you will have His pure freedom to walk in today.

I hope by now you see your quiet time with the Lord is a must if you're not spending time with my Lord you should repent. Please read the our Father and the next verses and notice six times Jesus said the word forgive

Matthew 6:9-15 After this manner therefore pray ye: Our Father which art in heaven, Hallowed be thy name. Thy kingdom come. Thy will be done in earth, as it is in heaven. Give us this day our daily bread. And *forgive* us our debts, as we *forgive* our debtors. And lead us not into temptation, but deliver us from evil: For thine is the kingdom, and the power, and the glory, forever. Amen. For if ye *forgive* men their trespasses, your heavenly Father will also *forgive* you: But if ye *forgive* not men their trespasses, neither will your Father *forgive* your trespasses.

I know Jesus has already laid down His life for my sin as an expression of His loving forgiveness to me. Maybe it was easier for Jesus to lay down His life for me than to let me see the hurt in his eyes caused by my sin. For me, the truth is Jesus loves me and it is His love that makes me want to keep His laws. I could truthfully say I don't want go to hell so I won't sin but more than the fear of going to hell. I fear seeing the hurt and distrust in the eyes of my loving Jesus and my Father. I truthfully want to only see Glory and joy in my Father's eyes when I stand before Jesus for judgment.

Just the thought of living my life selfishly for myself and forsaking all the love Jesus has for me; brings enough pain into my heart to make me want to go to hell if I were to sin and hurt my Jesus. I believe Jesus loves me so much I would rather go directly to hell then to see the hurt and distrust in His eyes caused by the pain of my sin of unbelief. I hope you see they did it all to prove their love for us and now it is simply our turn to prove we believe them.

I believe Jenny knew I loved her and in our forty years of marriage, Jenny never had to bring up her rules to me again. I looked at her right in her eyes and Jenny looked me right in my eyes and we both knew beyond any doubt we loved each other and I believe Jenny knew she was safe marrying me. I believe when I stand before Jesus for judgment that we will be looking each other in the eyes and the joy of our love for each other will brighten the heavens. This is my goal and Jesus makes all things possible because I simply believe He loves me.

This is why I believe so strongly in His forgiveness. Jesus has true forgiveness so we don't have to commit suicide to protect our loved one from doing something stupid, like hitting me with a pan. We are given everything we need to walk with Jesus. Jesus will even send an angel to help us if need be. Believe me when I say I would rather sweat blood and pray more earnestly to bring glory to my Jesus and my Father God than to waste one minute of their time by watching some stupid show on television. Come on people, we are commanded to be His love to everyone we meet. Being His love is not hard. Simply receive the love of Jesus to become the love of Jesus.

Becoming the love of Jesus isn't a hard walk. All it takes is denying our self to pick up our cross and follow Jesus. Are you listening for His voice or are you watching a rerun of *Everybody Loves Raymond?* We are all on a journey. Please listen for His voice. Lay down your life and pick up your cross and you will never worry about seeing the hurt in His eyes on your judgment day.

Jesus tells us how to live in Galatians 5:22-23:

Galatians 5:22-23   But the fruit of the Spirit is love, joy, peace, longsuffering, gentleness, goodness, faith, Meekness, temperance: *against such there is no law.*

When we accept the Holy Spirit of God into our hearts and live sowing all the fruits of the Holy Spirit and keep our thoughts focused on God, there is no need for law. Jenny needed to tell me her laws but our love for each other made breaking them almost impossible. It was not the punishment that kept me from breaking her laws. Our love and our respect for each other made my keeping her laws automatic. When my thoughts focused on Jenny, I seriously could never hurt her. Jesus needed to tell us His laws but our love and respect for each other makes breaking them almost impossible. When my thoughts focus on Jesus my whole world transforms around me.

Keep your focus on Jesus and you will know you are loved! Yes, keep all the law by keeping your focus on Jesus and His love for you will grow and over flow.

Where is Your Treasure?

I remember as a little boy I was going for walks with my siblings and my parents. We would walk down the street in our town where all the stores were. We would look in the store windows and dream of having what was on display there. My parents called it window shopping. I didn't realize it then but I was setting my eyes on a transistor radio in the store window and then focusing or dreaming of owning that radio. That whole summer, I focused on getting that radio. To earn the money I cut grass, caddied at a golf course, recycled papers, washed windows and did odd jobs around the neighborhood. Finally, I saved enough money to buy the transistor radio. I stayed focused all summer on earning enough money to buy the radio.

Jesus said in Luke 12:34:

Luke 12:34 For where your treasure is, there will your heart be also.

You know as a boy I focused my heart on a radio all summer. Now I know our one and only treasure above all treasures is our heart-to-heart relationship with my Jesus and Father God. Here on Earth, people will lay up treasures of gold. I read gold is pavement in heaven. Now I thank God for His unending grace towards me and for renewing my mind daily! Now if I take my focus off my Jesus I have the loving Holy Spirit of my Father and Jesus in me to help me return my focus on them. I have such joy walking with them and talking with them that I don't want to waste time doing things I used to hold dear.

Today, I don't seem to be distracted with the momentary junk of this world anymore. My treasure is in spending time with my Jesus. Jesus and Father God are my best friends. My focus is on having more intimate time with my best friends. By keeping my focus on my best friends, I live and walk in the presence of God. I receive understanding of their loving nature. Walking in the presence of God will open your eyes to see the needs of others and God Himself will give you way he wants to help others.

Jesus tells us in His Word that we are one with Him and the Father if we received their Holy Spirit in our heart. Then I go to church and hear people singing songs asking God to come down and fill this place. They sing 'Come Holy Spirit and bring your atmosphere.' I think to myself 'Do you believe any of the Word of God that says we have the Holy Spirit of Father God and Jesus in us now?' I have so much joy with Jesus. I mean, we set and have Coffee Time With Jesus every day. This is not an event in my life. Coffee Time With Jesus is every day. Jesus wakes me up every day and says, "Come on Ron it is time to get up so I make us some coffee and pour us a cup." Then we sit and talk, talk, talk. Jesus is my atmosphere and Jesus is always here.

So do we walk in the atmosphere or do we have to call it down? Let us ask Jesus how do we walk our walk with you Lord? We walk.

1 Peter 1:14-16 As obedient children, not fashioning yourselves according to the former lusts in your ignorance: But as he which hath called you is holy, so be ye holy in all manner of conversation; Because it is written, *Be ye holy; for I am holy*

I have never heard anyone call down holy. I mean I don't hear songs saying Jesus come fill our atmosphere with holy. I read here Jesus say, "It is written so it must be important; it is written, *Be ye holy; for I am holy.*"

We are blessed to have the Holy Spirit of God in us if we believe it. Our belief will empower us and enlighten us to ask Jesus to bring wisdom into our hearts so we can see ourselves as Jesus sees us – obedient children of His and not lusting after the junk of this world like we did in ignorance of our former selves. We will delight in our new relationship to God and our conversation will be transformed from meaningless worldly talk, into meaningful words edifying our Heavenly Father God and edifying one another

175

with holy conversation. Yes we will become Holy as He is Holy, the word says so and I believe Jesus.

1 Peter 1:17-19   And if ye call on the Father, who without respect of persons judgeth according to every man's work, pass the time of your sojourning here in fear: Forasmuch as ye know that ye were not redeemed with corruptible things, as silver and gold, from your vain conversation received by tradition from your fathers; But with the precious blood of Christ, as of a lamb without blemish and without spot:

Here Peter is telling us to call on our Father who without respect of persons judgeth according to everyman's work. This is so important to understand. Our Father God will judge us by what we do, not what our parents did or didn't do. We will stand alone for judgment. For me, this says the curses were broken by Jesus Christ if we believe and through belief we have new personal communication skills with our real Father through Jesus. Please allow this into your heart and you will no longer be burdened with the past but you will delight in your future following Jesus. You will become childish in your heart knowing you are loved by the ultimate lovers Jesus Christ and our Father God.

Then Peter goes on to say, "Pass the time of your sojourning *here* in fear: my one and only fear on this earth is allowing my thoughts to go into unbelief." The precious blood of Jesus, his praying in agony, and His steadfast love is what wakes me up every day and says you too can be free of the bondage of sin, cruses and hell that go with them. I believe and by choosing to stay focused on my Jesus I can live free. This freedom is for us all.

Forasmuch as ye know that ye were not redeemed with corruptible things, *as* silver and gold, or from your vain conversation *received* by tradition from your fathers. I believe Peter is saying no amount of silver and gold can buy your redemption and nothing can buy you freedom from the vain conversation spoken by your parents or grandparents except believing in the redemption blood of Jesus Christ. Nothing can buy you freedom from cruses and the like except believing Jesus paid the price with the blood of Jesus.

I believe Peter is telling us there is only one price for the redemption from the sin of unbelief. The ultimate sin is unbelief

176

and the ultimate price is paid by our belief in the precious blood of Jesus Christ, as of a lamb without blemish and a lamb without spot. We are made sinless and spotless and forgiven by simple belief. Jesus said so and I believe Jesus.

Again we are told we can walk a precious walk with my Jesus and the things our parents did or didn't do; no longer hold us in bondage. Our past has been lifted from us. Yes! Totally removed! Peter tells us we will need a healthy fear in our heart so our guard will be up and if the devil tries to bring up our past or put guilt on us by reminding us of our past or the past of our parents we need to remember we are redeemed by the precious blood of Christ. We are to prove our belief by our works and by our Godly conversation. Speak blessings over your children and watch God honor His word. Jesus paid the price to free us and I believe He did it because He loves me.

Remember our Father judges us all rightly by our walk, that is by the works we do and by our conversation. Please do not spend your time watching shows like *Gilligan's Island* reruns or sports etc which will lead us into useless conversations but guard what you put in your mind and heart and value your time here on earth. For our life is a gift from God, although there is no price to pay for our gift of life. I know we will answer to God how we consumed our life. Did we only do the things we were asked or did we go above and beyond what was ask of us?

We all know Jesus went above and beyond. Jesus is our example. Jesus listened to His Father everyday so let us plan to listen to His needs of today. Let us listen to be aware of who Jesus is putting in our path today. Let us listen for His guidance and let us be His hope and love to everyone as He was hope and love to everyone He met.

Read 1 Peter 1:18 again for it is so important. I believe we Christians have been taught bad information and we spend our time filling our minds and our houses with the dung of this world.

1 Peter 1:18 Forasmuch as ye know that ye were not redeemed with corruptible things, as silver and gold, from your vain conversation received by tradition from your fathers;

Here Peter calls silver and gold corruptible for it is corruptible and no amount of it will redeem your soul. If you are not focused on Our Lord your daily conversations will be vain conversations about the dung of this world. Vain conversations would include conversations about sports, politics, money, even pets, sex or any conversation that is not edifying our Lord and His love for us. These conversations take up our time and become bad especially when these conversations prove to everyone our focus is on these things and not our Lord.

1 Peter 1:19 But with the precious blood of Christ, as of a lamb without blemish and without spot

Here Peter is telling us our redemption was paid with the precious blood of Jesus Christ. His blood is a mighty big price tag so let our conversations, our focus, our walk, our life, our *treasure* become knowing Jesus intimately. Jesus is a lamb without blemish and without spot. We simply must focus on Jesus and what He needs done today for then we will not have useless conversations about the things of this world.

By keeping our mind focused on Jesus, we will be telling our dearest Jesus we appreciate the painful, bloody, sacrifice you made for us. When we focus our thoughts on Jesus we are telling Jesus we value Him more than the things of this world. We are telling Jesus you did enough, now we will follow you and worship you by keeping our walk, our conversations, our thoughts focused on you Lord. When we give up the things of this world, we are rewarded with freedom from our past. We will be rewarded with peace, joy, and the ability to love others like never before in our life. Now that's my Jesus! Yes the love of Jesus flowing through us is more joy then ten free new cars on your birthday

1 Peter 1:20-21 Who verily was foreordained before the foundation of the world, but was manifest in these last times for you, Who by him do believe in God, that raised him up from the dead, and gave him glory; that your faith and hope might be in God.

Because of Jesus, we do believe in God and the fact our Father God raised Jesus up from the dead, and gave Jesus glory that we may choose to have our faith, our hope and our belief in God. Yes our faith and our hope is in knowing Jesus was raised from the dead and so will we be raised from the dead. I believe Jesus never worried about His judgment day because Jesus never engaged in the things of this world, like piling up silver and gold in case he loses his job and Jesus never engaged in useless conversations. Jesus showed us we can hand our children the knowledge and understanding and wisdom that will lead them into a world of joy, peace, love and freedom from dung. That sure beats vain conversations of traditions of wisdom from man.

1 Peter 1:22-23 Seeing ye have purified your souls in obeying the truth through the Spirit unto unfeigned love of the brethren, see that ye love one another with a pure heart fervently: Being born again, not of corruptible seed, but of incorruptible, by the word of God, which liveth and abideth for ever.

You will have a purified heart when you listen to the Holy Spirit speaking in your heart and allow Him to flow His unfeigned love or unconditional love through you. The Holy Spirit will help you in your works and conversations. The goal is to see that ye love one another with a pure heart fervently. Then Peter tells us not to let our corruptible dung get in the way of receiving the love of God which liveth and abideth forever.

1 Peter 1:24-25 For all flesh is as grass, and all the glory of man as the flower of grass. The grass withereth, and the flower thereof falleth away: But the word of the Lord endureth for ever. And this is the word which by the gospel is preached unto you.

The Word of God will endure forever. We simply must stay focused on the example Jesus gave us. Jesus called our life here on earth a vapor of time and yet we have the ability to prove our belief in His love for us by our life, our conversations and our walk will bring Glory to God forever. Knowing our life is just a vapor of time should make giving up the momentary happiness of this world easy. Knowing we can please God with a vapor of time into an eternity reward of joy is the Good News. Please allow the Holy Spirit to talk to you, teach you, guide you in every decision we make for when we do we will become the unfeigned love of Jesus Christ to this world.

Remember there are so many voices bidding for your time. The voice of the devil will tell you earthly things will make you happy. Watch television, do drugs, lust after the flesh, lust after material junk etc, listen to the devil for a vapor of time he will occupy your time on these things, he will take your mind off the Joy of the Lord and get you focused on yourself, and momentary happiness, and dung. You have a choice, give the devil a vapor of time and the devil will gladly give you more hell then you can imagine.

Please set your mind on Jesus and don't let the devil get you focused on fighting these thoughts by trying not to sin. If you focus on trying not to sin you have your focus on the devil and sin. That is a win for the devil because your focus is not on God. I find I am no longer spending my time trying not to sin. I no longer think about how the devil is trying to come against me. In fact I focus on my best friends so much I don't think about the devil and his distractions any more. I believe Jesus is transforming me daily and I love who He is making me into. I simply choose to fix my mind on Jesus and the things He needs done today. I let Jesus set the agenda for my life by simply listening and discerning His voice. The fear of going to hell has been replaced with the Joy of the Lord being my strength and the price is I willingly give Jesus my vapor of time.

Remember we will all be eye to eye with Jesus someday and by the choices we make today we are choosing to see His love or the pain of our sins when we look into His eyes. Chose now to walk a precious walk with Jesus and be His love to everyone you meet for in doing so you will have a joyful judgment day. I believe when we look into the eyes of Jesus we will see HIS love, joy, peace, longsuffering, gentleness, goodness, faith Meekness, and temperance. And when Jesus sees these same fruits in our eyes looking at him the heavens will brighten because the Glory of God will have one more set of our eyes shining His love.

People are still asking the age old question, "Did Jesus fulfill the law?" To me the answer is a simple yes! Jesus fulfilled all the law because He said He did. Jesus said He came to fulfill the law and I believe Jesus did. For me, the question should be how do we fulfill the law? If you want to fulfill all the law simply believe you are loved. I believed Jenny loved me and Jenny believed I loved her. Our love for each other would not let us sin and hurt each other. I know Jesus loves me and Jesus knows I love Him. Our love for each other will not let me sin and hurt Him. Jesus died to prove His love for me and I will die to prove my love for Him. You will fulfill the law by making Jesus your best friend and you will never grieve Him with doubt.

What Does A Prayer of Faith Sound Like?

My wife Jenny knew for a fact that if she got sick I would do everything in my power to get her well. In our forty years of marriage and with sickness and health, Jenny never needed to ask me for help. Jenny never once said, "Please help me, Ron." Jenny and I knew we loved each other so we never needed to ask each other for help. Knowing we loved each other meant helping each other was automatic, not something you need to ask for or pray for or fast for and being there for each other was always our will and always our timing. Our love for each other formed our will and our timing to be the love for each other was now. The love of Jesus is perfect love so His perfect will is to help us and His perfect timing is now.

I believe our relationship with Jesus is the same way. I know Jesus loves me so I never need to ask Him for help if I get sick, I know healing is the will of Jesus so I know Jesus will heal me. When Paul was bitten by the poisonous snake, he shook it off and went back to eating. In Acts 28:1-6, He never asks God for protection from the poison. Paul had no fear and Paul never prayed for help. Remember that perfect love cast out fear. Jesus said it and I believe it. When David faced the giant, David never prayed to see if the fight was God's will, David never checked to see if it was the right timing of God but David was armed with faith in God and with faith David won the war in seconds. God wants to flow through you the same way.

The other morning I broke a tooth and somehow my broken tooth became infected. By the time I went to bed the right side of my face was swelled, my eye and my ear hurt to a point I couldn't lay on my right side. The pain kept me awake that night. I sang in songs to the Lord and thanked God for my recovery.

In the morning I had plans to see a couple in Pittsburg PA. The pain was bad enough that I wanted to call them and tell them I couldn't make it but in my heart I just knew Jesus would make everything all right. After a 90-minute drive, I arrived at my friend's house with no pain. At lunch time I didn't want to eat because I was afraid the pain would come back if food got in my tooth again. I was gently reminded by Jesus that I was in fear. I ate lunch and had dinner and we talked for fourteen hours. On the 90-minute ride back to my camper that night I sang praises to my Jesus for taking my pain and being so gentle with me about the fear of eating I had that morning.

You know I call Jesus my best friend. I call Jesus *my Jesus*. I tell everyone I am the favorite of Jesus and I know I am His favorite. I tell everyone how much hearing from Jesus means to me and I tell everyone how I start my day with these simple words, "Dearest Jesus what are we going to do today?" But in my heart I wish I really could describe our love for each other. I just run out of words. I love you too, Jesus!

Do you remember when Jesus told the apostles that faith the size of a mustard seed could move a mountain?

Matthew 17:20 And Jesus said unto them, Because of your unbelief: for verily I say unto you, If ye have faith as a grain of mustard seed, ye shall say unto this mountain, Remove hence to yonder place; and it shall remove; and nothing shall be impossible unto you.

Notice that Jesus didn't say pray and ask me to move the mountain. Jesus didn't say pray and tell me about the problem. Jesus didn't say if the timing is right I'll move it for you or if it is my will I might move it for you. Jesus didn't say go to church and get some loud music going to get me in the mood then call down my Holy Spirit and maybe I'll move the mountain. I believe Jesus was saying even a tiny mustard seed of faith in you is enough faith for Jesus to move a mountain.

Let us look at one of the mountains Paul had and how Paul handled it:

Acts 28:3-6 And when Paul had gathered a bundle of sticks, and laid them on the fire, there came a viper out of the heat, and fastened on his hand. And when the barbarians saw the venomous beast hang on his hand, they said among themselves, No doubt this man is a murderer, whom, though he hath escaped the sea, yet vengeance suffereth not to live. And he shook off the beast into the fire, and felt no harm. Howbeit they looked when he should have swollen, or fallen down dead suddenly: but after they had looked a great while, and saw no harm come to him, they changed their minds, and said that he was a god.

When I read this passage, I told God I want faith like that of Paul's. I mean, when the poisonous snake bites me I don't want to run to Jesus in fear screaming for help like God didn't know a snake bit me. I want to go on about the work God has for me and not even give the devil of fear any of my time that day. Sometimes, a prayer of faith is a no prayer at all. Paul did not pray. If you know you are loved by God already, you will walk in faith because you know you are loved. Knowing you are loved by Jesus makes healing, protection, deliverance and anything you need automatic. Praise Father God and Jesus for the wisdom of being loved and praise them your name is written in heaven! Remember to praise God in faith knowing God has an answer and God is the answer and God did answer.

A couple nights ago, I went to my brother's house for dinner. Bob's wife Sally is a great cook and she lived up to her reputation again that night. They gave me a little devotional prayer book. I usually don't do devotional readings because I let Jesus set the topic of the day. For some reason I felt prompted to start reading through this one.

There was one devotional titled *God Who Provides*. It was a story about a dad asking his little girl why she didn't make a Christmas list this year. Dad asked her, "Don't you believe in Santa?" The little girl answered, "Oh yes I believe! But if I write and tell him what I want, I'll never know what he just wanted to give me."

I pray for all to have the faith that we don't need to ask God for anything. Instead we just know God has already provided everything. Sometimes no list is the best list. Sometimes a prayer of faith is no prayer at all, just stand in faith.

We Must Know Jesus as Our Source

A while ago, I sat in a Christian class room where the students were learning how to handle situations they were probably going to encounter as Christian teachers in a public school. They were given ten detailed ways to handle a problem. The instructor then asks his students if they had any questions. I was a guest for the day but was given permission to participate. So I asked, "What to do if you use all ten solutions and haven't solved the problem?"

They didn't have an answer because their solutions were so well-thought out and on target they were sure they had the problem solved. I said, "I believe there is one more solution. I believe the first of the ten solutions should be to go to our source, Jesus Christ. Jesus will always have an answer and if we go to him first we are putting our trust in God instead of ourselves and we will have the best solution, first. We Christians really need to know Jesus as our first source and really need to know Jesus is our only source. Jesus loves faith and faith moves the mountain so put your faith in God, for it is God who solves the problem. Jesus said it and I believe it."

In our walk with Jesus, we simply must seek God with our whole heart. We must know our name is written in Heaven and we will know our name is written in Heaven if we have a personal loving relationship with Jesus. The first time I heard Jesus call me by name I almost jumped out of my skin! Jesus is alive and He knows me. Jesus is real and He loves me. Jesus will treat you as His best friend because you are. Walk and talk with my Jesus daily and you will never regret it. Put your faith in Him to have an answer and you will know you have the answer.

Walk in faith, talk in faith, and live in faith by knowing that you know Jesus is dwelling in you. Having the Holy Spirit in you means you have been sealed by His love. So walk in His love.

I spent the entire summer of 2014 in California. By the end of summer, I was pretty exhausted and found myself asking God for a break. I just wanted some time to recharge and really I just wanted to be totally alone with my Jesus. Everywhere I went, there was work to do. I was driving toward Oklahoma City when the blower motor in the motor home quit working so I had no heat and it was freezing cold out.

I asked God to find me a campground and He did. I plugged in and got the heat on in my camper. I bought a new blower motor and installed it. And no sooner I finished the repair and the phone rang. A friend from Ohio called to ask where I was. Upon telling him that I was at Oklahoma City he said, "I have a daughter there and I would like for you could spend some time with her." A couple minutes later, Paula called from California and her sister had a sister in Oklahoma City who would like for us to spend time together. Within minutes, a third call came in and suddenly I had three appointments to meet people. I spent five glorious days in Oklahoma City.

At 5:30 P.M. on Friday night, I arrived at my first appointment. We talked until 6:45 A.M. Yes, more than 12 hours! Really it seemed we just talked in ten minutes. I had another appointment to meet the second couple at 11:30 that morning. By the time I got back to my camper and showered I had less than 2 hours to sleep before my next meeting. I reminded God I have been up over 24 hours straight and I don't have an alarm clock so make sure I am up in time to make my next appointment. Looking back on that request, I think I heard God say as I went to sleep, "Oh ye of little faith." God not only got me up in time but I was refreshed and felt great. The meeting went great but we didn't have enough time together so we decided to meet and go to church together on Sunday and talk some more afterward.

The other couple I had planned to meet on Sunday graciously allowed me to reset the time for our Sunday visit with them to Monday. Sunday went better than great and Monday's visit was really fruitful also. On Tuesday, I headed for Tennessee. On the way, I prayed and asked God for some one-on-one time again. I prayed, "Please dear Jesus, I miss you and I thank you Jesus we will have some one on one time together."

I arrived at one of my free campgrounds in Tennessee. I am a member of Thousand Trails so I can camp for free. The girl came to the office to check me in. She asked me, "How many days do you want to stay?" I was thinking I would stay one night but ten came out of my mouth. As she was typing the information I turned my head and looked around the empty office for Jesus and said out loud, "Ten? Are you sure ten? Just then the girl said, "I heard you the first time." I looked at her and said, "I was not talking to you." Because I had talked out loud and there was no one else in the office, she looked at me like I was weird. Mom, go figure.

I drove into the campground to find a campsite. The campground was huge. I realized I was the only one there. After setting up and having some Coffee Time With Jesus, I thought to myself, "No one is here so no one is going to invite me for dinner. I better go and buy some food." Jenny's chilly came into my mind. I hadn't made her chilly in forever.

That night, I continued writing the *One Heart at a Time* book until 10:30 P.M. when I went to bed. As soon as I put my head on the pillow I heard the words, "You know it is going to rain tomorrow." I knew exactly what Jesus was talking about. I had bought the fixings for Jenny's homemade chilly but if you cook chilly in the camper the camper smells like chilly for what seems like a week. It was 68 degrees out so I got up and put the fixings in a pot on an electric burner outside.

Also that day, I had found some old CD's and started playing one on the outside radio. A song came on and the words were 'I'm not looking for a hole in the ground; I'm looking for a hole in the sky. I'm not looking for a place to land; I'm looking for a place to fly. Jesus loves me and let me tell you why.' I put the radio on repeat and I was singing out loud. Every time the song came to the words 'I'm looking for a place to fly' I was on top the picnic table and I would jump off with my hands held high and scream, "I'm looking for a place to fly! Jesus loves me and let me tell you why!"

I was having so much fun when all of a sudden I saw two people standing over by the street light. I turned off my radio and asked them, "How long have you two been standing there?" After they stopped laughing they answered, "About a half hour." I was in shocked to see someone out that late but I managed to invite them over to my camper but for some reason, they declined. I asked them where they came from because I knew I was the only one in the campground. They told me they arrived late and where only staying one night so they picked a site down by the entrance to the campground.

They also thought they were the only ones in the campground. Around ten o'clock they listened to the weather and decided to go for a walk having heard the weatherman predict rain for the next day. She told me they were walking when they heard loud music and decided to see where the party was. I guess to them it looked like a one-man party until they got closer and saw Jesus and I having so much fun.

I spent ten glorious days with my Jesus that I will never forget. I felt like I was on vacation with my Jesus. I pray for more time and I look so forward to when Jesus and I are fulltime. Today though, we have work to do and I depended on Jesus to prompt me and then give me His words and His actions so together we will see His work completed. I don't rush. I don't feel pressured. I don't worry because I know I am loved by the lover of my soul and together we have a great walk. Do you? I pray that you do!

Is God Supernatural?

YES! God is supernatural and spectacular. I have met people that have had some supernatural experiences. Last night, I watched one of these supernatural testimonies on a DVD that a friend gave me. After it was over, I wondered if I had just wasted an hour and a half of my life. The man giving the testimony was sincere to the max. He was trustworthy and on fire for God. I talked to my Jesus about this man's testimony and Jesus asked me, "Ron you are having a problem with his testimony because there is nothing in my word to verify his vision?" I thank you Jesus for making me understands! I mean I wasn't sure why I felt the way I did and Jesus clarified my thoughts for me.

I know people that seek to have their own supernatural experience with God. They will fast for breakthrough and tell me how they feel they are going to get this supernatural experience real soon. Some of these people go to churches that have a reputation for calling down the Holy Spirit. They are excited to tell everyone about 'their supernatural encounters with God.' I pray for God to give me the words to help them seek first the kingdom of God. For when they do, they will walk in the supernatural experiences of God daily.

I read in my Holy Bible we are to seek God with all your heart, and all your spirit.

Matthew 6:33   But seek ye first the kingdom of God, and his righteousness; and all these things shall be added unto you.

Deuteronomy 4:29 But from there you will seek the LORD your God and you will find him, if you search after him with all your heart and with all your soul.

I read we are to become the love of Jesus Christ to everyone we meet. I read that we are His ambassadors and as such we are to heal the sick, cast out devils and raise the dead. I read we can listen to the voice of God and have a daily personal relationship with Jesus. I read how to discern the voice of God. I read we have their Holy Spirit in us. I read we can talk in tongues. I read we have the gifts of the Holy Spirit in us. I could go on and on about my Jesus and my daily walk with Him. I believe if I fast and pray and seek the supernatural experience. I just might miss the *Joy of a daily* walk with my Jesus holding my hand.

I believe a supernatural experience would be great and if I have one and if Jesus shows me how to prove it is real in the Scriptures, I will let the world know about it. I believe they do happen. I mean, Jesus said all things are possible and I believe Jesus. The man who gave his testimony about his supernatural experiences never did not say he prayed for nor did he fast to get one. I just do not pray for one and I do not seek one and I do not fast to have one. I haven't read in the Holy Bible to seek ye first the supernatural experience; but if one comes along and I experience it. Well then, glory to God I will share it.

When Jesus walked this earth with the apostles, the apostles experienced the supernatural every day. Think about that. They didn't fast, beg, cry out to the Lord and they were not even born again. The supernatural experience was Jesus being Jesus. The apostles knew Jesus had something they wanted and Jesus gave them the gifts they wanted.

When Jesus had sent them out to preach, they came back very excited to tell Jesus about how they operated in the gift of calling on his name and saw the supernatural. Jesus has a supernatural gift for each one of us. Actually Jesus is the supernatural gift for each one of us and Jesus gave us the gift of being born into the Kingdom of God, adopted into His bloodline. Jesus gave us His power and authority on the Earth, Jesus removed our past by renewing our minds. Jesus broke all the curses handed down by adopting us into a supernatural bloodline and gives a future that is so supernatural. I want everyone I meet to experience God personally like I have and like the apostles did. Jesus said all things are possible. I believe the supernatural to us is natural to God. To me it seems natural to believe Him.

Choosing To Be With God!

I want to thank you for reading this book. I pray you are inspired to have this personal relationship with my Jesus. I pray this book brings you closer to my Jesus and is a helpful guide to seeking the Lord. Remember to preach the Kingdom of God is at hand because you are there. Remember, the most powerful revelation on Earth is God loves you. Remember, you have the Holy Spirit of Father God and Jesus in you 24/7 so talk to them 24/7. Use the revelation of being loved by God as your starting point and watch God bring everything else into focus for you. All things are possible for you when you know you are loved by God.

Make listening to the voice of God your biggest priority by turning off the distractions, no matter how interesting or how funny they are. This is simply a must. Remember when you are standing in front of the magistrate Jesus will give you the words to help the magistrate for Jesus said:

Luke 12:11-12 And when they bring you unto the synagogues, and unto magistrates, and powers, take ye no thought how or what thing ye shall answer, or what ye shall say: For the Holy Ghost shall teach you in the same hour what ye ought to say.

I ask my Jesus in my Coffee Time With Jesus, who is the magistrate to me. I mean, I have never been called before a governor or person of authority to defend my faith, so Jesus told me who my magistrate is? Jesus said, "Anyone I put before you Ron." Again, Jesus makes all things simple for me because I know I am loved. Now I never worry about what to say in any situation because by faith I know Jesus will give me the words to help anyone He puts in front of me. Want confirmation?

Mark 13:11 But when they shall lead you, and deliver you up, take no thought beforehand what ye shall speak, neither do ye premeditate: but whatsoever shall be given you in that hour, that speak ye: for it is not ye that speak, but the Holy Ghost.

Yes, Jesus said it and I believe it. Jesus lives right inside of you so go and enjoy your walk. I believe if you keep your focus on God, God will focus on you. Come as a child to God and see results that will bewilder an adult. Keep your focus on God and His future for you and the devil of your past will flee.

One more comment before closing. The house I built for Jenny and our family was setting on five acres. It was a pan handle lot, so are drive way was two tents of a mile long. You couldn't see another house from our house. We were in big woods so we never had curtains in our windows. In the spring, I loved getting up early and having coffee on the deck while listening to everything wakes up. You could hear everything. The birds singing, deer walking, squirrels chirping, all kinds of animals playing, I loved being there.

I noticed when I got up to late I would miss this beautiful quiet time. It seemed when the sun came up a little higher the nature sounds faded and the noise of the day filled my ears. I would see the grass needed cut and the flowers needed weeding. The work of the day would fill my head and all of God's creation got quiet. I knew the sounds were still there but hearing them became difficult to impossible.

Now I wake up and Jesus and I talk. I truly love this quiet time with my Jesus. Knowing Jesus calls me by name is wonderful. Jesus tells me, I am His presence 24/7 and He loves making me shine. I ask my Jesus every day, "What are we going to do today?" and Jesus has the same answer every day. Jesus says, "Ron simply be my love to everyone you meet today." Please make quiet time to listen for His voice and when you do give of your time you will find the rest of the world is on hold. You will not be late for anything. You will not rush, you will not worry, and you will have peace and joy unspeakable. You will find the voice of Jesus is even better then all nature sounds combined.

Now that's my Jesus and He loves me. This I know because He wakes me up every morning to tell me so. Jesus wipes the sleep out of my eyes and says, "Come on Ron, it is time to get up." So I make us some coffee and pour us a cup. Then we sit and talk, talk, talk. Now that is my Jesus way to wake up.

Now please go in peace and walk daily knowing and believing

Ephesians 1:13-17 In him you also, when you heard the word of truth, the gospel of your salvation, and believed in him, were sealed with the promised Holy Spirit, who is the guarantee of our inheritance until we acquire possession of it, to the praise of his glory. For this reason, because I have heard of your faith in the Lord Jesus and your love toward all the saints, I do not cease to give thanks for you, remembering you in my prayers, that the God of our Lord Jesus Christ, the Father of glory, may give you the Spirit of wisdom and of revelation in the knowledge of him,

I pray for you to have a supernatural personal relationship with Jesus also. To have a personal walk with my Jesus, remember that in Psalms 46:10 "Be still, and know that I am God. I will be exalted among the nations; I will be exalted in the earth!"

Be still and know God is being exalted in your heart to all the nations and in the earth.

BEING STILL AND
LOVING MY JESUS

Jenny, Ron and my Jesus

Well here is the hook:

Ephesians 1:17 that the God of our Lord Jesus Christ, the Father of glory, may give you the Spirit of wisdom and of revelation in the knowledge of him,

Paul wrote to the Ephesians and I believe it is for us also. To hear from God, we must have some quiet time. As you read this book you will recognize the things of this world as worthless compared to the joy and peace of knowing Jesus knows you on a first name basis. I prayed and I have asked my Jesus to let this book give the reader a desire to be intimately in love with the one who loves us. Jesus is waiting quietly to bring you into His joy by giving you the *Spirit of wisdom and of revelation in the knowledge of him.*

Luke 12:11-12 And when they bring you unto the synagogues, and unto magistrates, and powers, take ye no thought how or what thing ye shall answer, or what ye shall say: For the Holy Ghost shall teach you in the same hour what ye ought to say.

In my quiet time with Jesus I ask him, who is the magistrate to me. I mean, I have never been called before a governor or person of authority to defend my faith. Jesus told me who my magistrate is? Jesus said, "Anyone I put before you Ron." Again Jesus makes all things simple for me because I know I am loved. Now I never worry about what to say in any situation because by faith I know Jesus will give me the words to help anyone He puts in front of me. Want confirmation?

Mark 13:11 But when they shall lead you, and deliver you up, take no thought beforehand what ye shall speak, neither do ye premeditate: but whatsoever shall be given you in that hour, that speak ye: for it is not ye that speak, but the Holy Ghost.

This is true peace, true hope for your family, friends and nation and it comes gift rapped in the true love of my Jesus.

Thank you for reading this book and God bless you and all your loved ones!

Made in the USA
Middletown, DE
16 June 2016